A CHILD'S INTRODUCTION TO

ASIAN AMERICAN AND PACIFIC ISLANDER HISTORY

A CHILD'S INTRODUCTION TO

ASIAN AMERICAN AND PACIFIC ISLANDER HISTORY

The Heroes, the Stories, and the Cultures that Helped to Build America

NAOMI HIRAHARA

Illustrated by SARAH DEMONTEVERDE

BLACK DOG
& LEVENTHAL
PUBLISHERS
NEW YORK

Black Dog & Leventhal Publishers
Hachette Book Group
1290 Avenue of the Americas
New York, NY 10104

Distributed in the United Kingdom by Little, Brown Book Group UK, Carmelite House,
50 Victoria Embankment, London, EC4Y 0DZ

www.hachettebookgroup.com
www.blackdogandleventhal.com
 BlackDogandLeventhal @BDLev

First Edition: April 2024

Published by Black Dog & Leventhal Publishers, an imprint of Hachette Book Group, Inc.
The Black Dog & Leventhal Publishers name and logo are trademarks of Hachette Book Group, Inc.

The publisher is not responsible for websites (or their content) that are not owned by the publisher.

The Hachette Speakers Bureau provides a wide range of authors for speaking events.
To find out more, go to hachettespeakersbureau.com or email HachetteSpeakers@hbgusa.com.

Black Dog & Leventhal books may be purchased in bulk for business, educational, or promotional use.
For more information, please contact your local bookseller or the Hachette Book Group Special Markets Department at Special.Markets@hbgusa.com.

Print book interior design by Katie Benezra

Library of Congress Cataloging-in-Publication Data

Names: Hirahara, Naomi, 1962– author. | Demonteverde, Sarah, illustrator.
Title: A child's introduction to Asian American and Pacific Islander history : the heroes, the stories,
    and the cultures that helped to build America / Naomi Hirahara, Sarah Demonteverde.
Other titles: Child's introduction to AAPI history
Description: First edition. | New York : Black Dog & Leventhal, 2024. | Includes bibliographical references and index.
Audience: Ages 8–12
Summary: "Celebrate the diversity, history, and rich culture of the Asian American and Pacific Islander community
    and teach kids ages 8–12 about the people, experiences, and events that have shaped AAPI history" —Provided
    by publisher.
Identifiers: LCCN 2023007138 (print) | LCCN 2023007139 (ebook) | ISBN 9780762483969 (hardcover) | ISBN
    9780762483976 (ebook)
Subjects: LCSH: Asian Americans—History—Juvenile works. | Pacific Islander Americans—History—Juvenile works.
Classification: LCC E184.A75 .H573 2024 (print) | LCC E184.A75 (ebook) | DDC 973/.0495—dc23/eng/20230221
    LC record available at https://lccn.loc.gov/2023007138
    LC ebook record available at https://lccn.loc.gov/2023007139

ISBNs: 978-0-7624-8396-9 (hardcover); 978-0-7624-8397-6 (ebook)

Printed in Thailand

PCF

10 9 8 7 6 5 4 3 2

CONTENTS

WHO ARE ASIAN AMERICANS AND PACIFIC ISLANDERS?

You may have heard the phrase "Asian American" before. But what does that mean? Who are Asian Americans? Is a Chinese immigrant who came from a small village in China in the mid-1800s to search for gold in California considered an Asian American? How about a Muslim Indian movie producer who lives in New York City? Or a mixed-race Japanese American with a non-Asian name whose great-grandparents came to the United States from a small farming village in southern Japan?

The first people to use the phrase "Asian American" were two college students in 1968. **Yuji Ichioka** and **Emma Gee** saw that people who came from or whose family came from Asian countries faced racism and discrimination because of the color of their skin. At the time, Black leaders in the United States were fighting for equal rights. Yuji and Emma were inspired by them and thought people of Asian descent needed to band together.

In the beginning, mostly people with roots from countries like China, Japan, and Korea were seen as Asian Americans. Many people from the Philippines are of Asian and Latino ancestry and were also included, but sometimes Filipinos wanted to be seen as separate. Later, people from other countries like Vietnam and India began coming to the United States, and they were also included under the phrase "Asian Americans."

West Asians, such as those people from Iran, Iraq, Lebanon, Saudi Arabia, and Turkey, have been classified by the US government as white but some organizations consider them

AAPI: A shortened term for "Asian American and Pacific Islander"

Ancestry/Roots: Where past relatives are from

Discrimination: Being unfair to a person or group of people because of their race or ethnicity

Emigrant: A person who leaves a country of birth

Emigration: Leaving a country of birth

Immigrant: A person who has moved to a new country

Immigration: Moving to a new country

Indigenous: The first people to live in a certain place in the world. For example, Native Hawaiians are indigenous to Hawai'i.

Mixed Race: Of two or more races

Refugees: People who must escape to another country because of war or other hardship

Segregated: Separated by race or ethnicity. For example, a Chinese segregated school only has students of Chinese descent.

Territory: An area of land (in this book, usually an island or group of islands) under the control of a nation like the United States

to be Asian American. Some with these roots prefer the phrase "Middle Eastern." As you can see, there is not one definition of who is an Asian American. We have included people with roots in East Asia, Southeast Asia, and South Asia, but not Central or West Asia.

Another term you may have heard is "Pacific Islanders." These are people from native or indigenous populations on thousands of islands throughout the Pacific Ocean. Their origin story is very different than immigrants from Asian countries and their children and

grandchildren, so they fought for a distinct name: Pacific Islander.

You may be wondering what ties Asian Americans with Pacific Islanders. It begins with crossing the Pacific Ocean.

POPULATION FACT

About 24 million people in the United States identify as being Asian while 1.7 million people identify as Native Hawaiian or Pacific Islander.

MAPS OF ASIA AND THE PACIFIC ISLANDS

These maps of Asia and the Pacific Islands will help you learn where the different groups and people in this book came from. The map of Asia is divided into East Asia, Southeast Asia, and South Asia. The Pacific Islands are part of Oceania, which includes more than ten thousand islands in the Pacific Ocean. Polynesia is an island group that includes Hawai'i, Sāmoa, Tonga, and New Zealand.

WHAT DO YOU CALL A PERSON FROM A CERTAIN COUNTRY IN ASIA OR THE PACIFIC ISLANDS?

1. **Bangladesh:** Bangladeshi

2. **Bhutan:** Bhutanese

3. **Myanmar (also called Burma):** Myanmarese and Burmese

4. **Cambodia:** Cambodian

5. **China:** Chinese

6. **India:** Indian

7. **Indonesia:** Indonesian

8. **Japan:** Japanese

9. **North Korea** and **South Korea:** Korean

10. **Laos:** Laotian

11. **Malaysia:** Malaysian

12. **Maldives:** Maldivian

13. **Mongolia:** Mongolian

14. **Nepal:** Nepalese

15. **Pakistan:** Pakistani

16. **Philippines:** Filipino

17. **Singapore:** Singaporean

18. **Sri Lanka:** Sri Lankan

19. **Taiwan:** Taiwanese

20. **Thailand:** Thai

21. **Vietnam:** Vietnamese

SOME PACIFIC ISLANDS

22. **Guam:** Guamanian or CHamoru (preferred by native people)

23. **Kiribati:** I-Kiribati

24. **Marshall Islands:** Marshallese

25. **Palau:** Palauan

26. **Sāmoa:** Samoan

27. **Tonga:** Tongan

ASIAN AMERICAN AND PACIFIC ISLANDER COMMUNITIES IN THE UNITED STATES

Most Asian Americans and Pacific Islanders live in Hawai'i, California, New York, New Jersey, Boston, and Chicago, but there have been pockets of various ethnic groups throughout the United States.

MARSHALLESE
in Springdale, Arkansas

. . . .

Half of the Marshallese population in the United States lives in Springdale, Arkansas, in the center of the Ozark Mountains. Marshallese people are from the Marshall Islands, a country of more than 1,200 islands in the eastern part of Micronesia. Japan ruled these islands before 1945, but after the end of World War II, the Marshall Islands became a US-controlled trust territory from 1947 to 1986. Under the trust territory rules, Marshallese individuals could not freely travel to the United States unless they were students in an American school, like a college.

John Moody was one of the first Marshallese people to move to Springdale in 1986. He came to the United States as a student but then worked in a factory where they raised chickens. People in the Marshall Islands heard there were jobs in Springdale. More than fifteen thousand Marshallese now live in Springdale and other cities in the states of Arkansas, Oklahoma, Kansas, and Missouri.

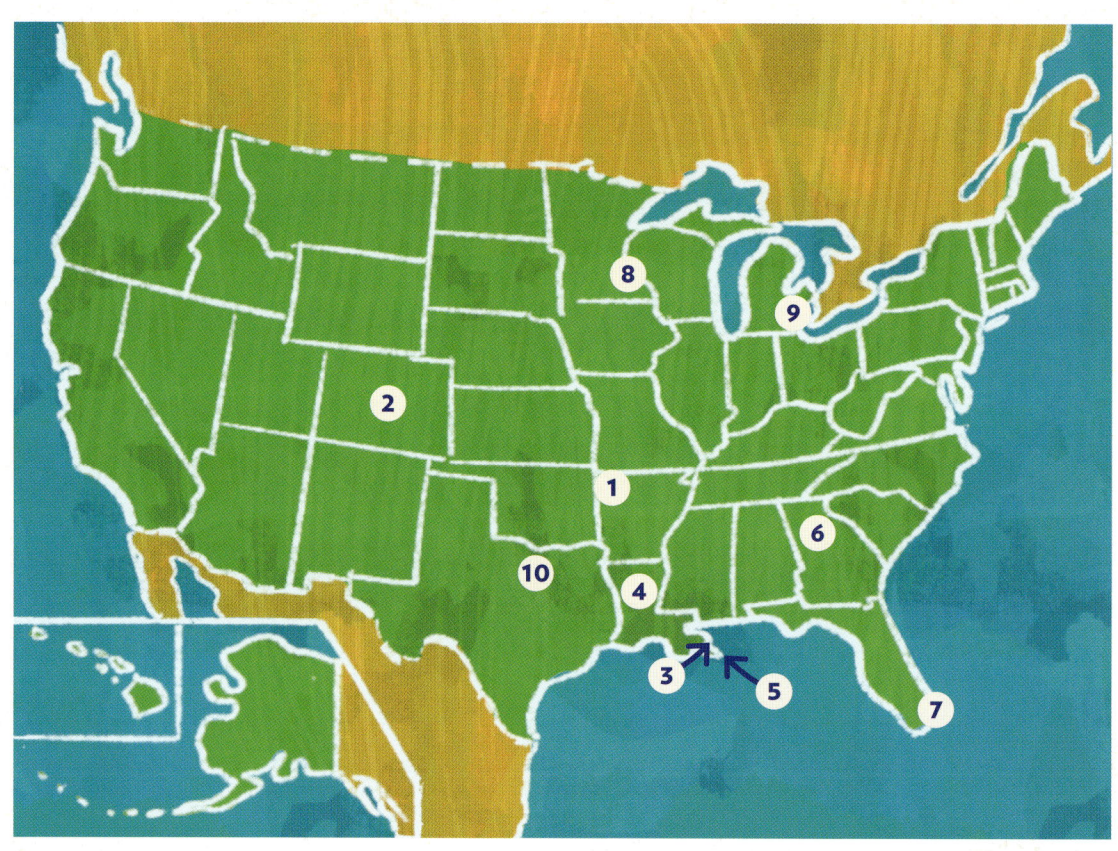

1. Springdale, Arkansas
2. Colorado Rockies
3. St. Malo, Louisiana
4. Louisiana
5. Mississippi Delta
6. Gwinett County, Georgia
7. Boca Raton, Florida
8. Twin Cities
9. Hamtramck, Michigan
10. Plano, Texas

A Filipino fisherman in St. Malo, Louisiana

TIBETANS
in the Colorado Rockies

Colorado is home to four hundred Tibetan Americans. Most of them live in the cities of Denver, Broomfield, and Boulder. Tibetan immigrants feel at home near the Colorado Rockies because they are surrounded by mountains, just like their homes in Tibet. Tibet is called "the Roof of the World" for its high mountains, including Mount Everest, which is shared with the country of Nepal. Tibetans first arrived in the Rocky Mountain region in the 1950s as secret agents for the CIA in India and Nepal. They trained at Colorado's Camp Hale, which became a national monument in 2022.

FILIPINOS
in St. Malo, Louisiana

Asian American history in the United States goes back hundreds of years. Its beginning can be traced to a small fishing village in Louisiana called St. Malo. When Spain took over Louisiana from the French in 1763, Filipinos made their way to Louisiana, where people spoke Spanish and were followers of Catholicism. Filipino fishermen found success in getting shrimp in the Delta. Native Americans and escaped slaves called the Maroons were the first to settle in St. Malo.

VIETNAMESE SHRIMPERS
in Louisiana

Today, Vietnamese refugees are about one-quarter of Louisiana's shrimpers. Shrimpers are fishermen who catch shrimp. When the Vietnamese first arrived in 1975, they liked the warm weather, which was similar to the weather in Vietnam. The state's Catholic community was especially welcoming of the refugees, many of whom were also Catholics. More than seventeen thousand Vietnamese Americans live in the New Orleans area today.

A Chinese grocery store in the Mississippi Delta

CHINESE
in the Mississippi Delta
· ·

At one time, there were fifty groceries run by Chinese families in the Mississippi Delta town of Greenville. A delta is the area around a river. Chinese immigrants first picked cotton in the Mississippi Delta in the 1800s but quickly switched to opening stores in their communities. In 1968, **Suey "Henry" Heong Wong** opened up Greenville's first Chinese restaurant, serving butterfly shrimp, chow mein, and chop suey. In the 1970s, there were 2,500 people of Chinese descent living in the Mississippi Delta region.

KOREANS
in Gwinnett County, Georgia
· ·

Gwinnett County, Georgia, is near the city of Atlanta. It is known as "Seoul of the South" because of its large and growing Korean American population. Koreans first started moving into the county of Gwinnett in the late 1980s and early 1990s. They opened restaurants and churches. The county even has a Korean-language television station and ten Korean-language newspapers. Koreans are attracted to Gwinnett for its schools, its similar climate to Seoul, good transportation, and even its familiar red dirt.

A Korean-language newspaper from Gwinnett County, Georgia

JAPANESE
in Boca Raton, Florida

In the summer of 1905, more than a dozen Japanese settlers led by **Jo Sakai** (1874–1923) founded a farming colony in the Boca Raton area of Florida. They called their community Yamato Colony, in honor of their Japanese roots. Five years earlier, there was only one resident of Japanese ancestry in the whole state of Florida. The colony never grew to more than forty people. While they had some success with tomato and pineapple crops, the colony fell apart through the 1920s and 1930s. The longest surviving pioneering settler, **Sukeji "George" Morikami** (1886–1976), continued to farm in the area and eventually donated nearly two hundred acres of land to Palm Beach County, leading to the creation of the Morikami Museum and Gardens in Delray Beach, Florida.

Sukeji "George" Morikami on his farm in Boca Raton, Florida

HMONG
in the Twin Cities, Minnesota

The Twin Cities region of Minnesota has the largest concentration of Hmong in the United States. The Hmong are a group of people with roots in China who eventually settled in the mountains of the countries of Laos, Myanmar (also called Burma), Thailand, and Vietnam. More than nineteen thousand men in Laos were spies for the United States in a civil war within Southeast Asia. Many Hmong died in the war, and others fled to countries like Thailand. Eventually, the first Hmong family arrived in Minnesota in 1975, and churches helped other families come to the Twin Cities. Today, more than eighty-five thousand Hmong live in the area.

BANGLADESHIS
in Hamtramck, Michigan

About one-quarter of the 22,500 residents of the town of Hamtramck, Michigan, near Detroit, are of Bangladeshi ancestry. Bangladesh was known as East Pakistan when members of the group began to come to Detroit in the 1960s. Many Bangladeshis, like other immigrants, first came to work for Detroit's car industry. More came to Hamtramck in the early 2000s when Bangladeshi Americans relocated from New York City to Michigan for a better quality of life. Most people from Bangladesh practice Islam. In 2021, a Muslim mayor was voted into office.

ASIAN AMERICANS
in Plano, Texas

Almost 25 percent of the people in the city of Plano, Texas, are of Asian descent. Chinese railroad workers first came to Texas from California in 1870. When the Chinese Exclusion Act was repealed in 1943, professionals from northern and central China as well as college students from Taiwan began to enter cities like Plano. (We'll learn more about this act on page 28.) The populations increased when large employers like Toyota Motors moved their headquarters to Plano. Today, more than twelve thousand of the fifty thousand students who attend Plano public schools are of Asian descent. The larger Plano region has more than fifteen grocery stores that sell foodstuffs for Chinese, South Asian, Korean, Japanese, Vietnamese, and Thai dishes.

FROM THE PACIFIC: EARLY IMMIGRATION

Thousands of years before the United States of America was a country, people lived in Oceania. Oceania refers to most of the islands scattered throughout the Pacific Ocean (see map on pages 8–9). Some arrived by foot from northern Australia before the remote lands were surrounded by water and became islands. Others traveled to the islands from Asia in outrigger canoes, depending only on the observation of the sea, sky, and stars to navigate through the waters. This ancient navigation tradition was passed on from generation to generation.

WAYFINDING IN OCEANIA

Mau Piailug (1932–2010) was one year old when his grandfather, an experienced wayfinder, took him to tide pools and taught him to watch the effects of the wind on the movement of water. Wayfinding is an ancient way of navigating, or finding your way by observing the water, the stars, and the wind. They were on the small Micronesian island of Satawal, which was only a mile and a half long. Mau eventually was declared a master navigator like his grandfather. Traditionally, those who were not living in Micronesia could not be wayfinders. But Mau decided to help others travel from Tahiti to Hawaiʻi by observing the water.

HULA DANCING

Another traditional master is **Edith Kanakaʻole** (1913–1979), who was known as "Aunty Edith." She was born on Hawaiʻi's Big Island and grew up speaking the Hawaiian language. She became a famous hula dancer. Hula was created by Polynesians, who were the first people who settled in Hawaiʻi. Aunty

Mau Piailug wayfinding in Satawal

Edith was committed to embracing oli (native chants) and the hula of her heritage, which formed the foundations of moʻolelo, or stories, that were in danger of being lost due to colonization. She opened her own hālua (hula school) in 1953 and traveled around the United States and Asia to perform hula that she choreographed to accompany her original oli. In the 1970s, people became more interested in native cultures on the islands. This was called the Hawaiian Renaissance. Aunty Edith helped create the first Hawaiian language program for public school students and created college courses on Polynesian history and the arts. She received the Distinction of Cultural Leadership award, the state's highest honor, in 1979. She was featured on the US quarter in 2023 as part of the American Women Quarters program.

COLONIZATION

The history of the islands in the Pacific Ocean is complicated. Other countries, like the United States and Japan, would come to different islands and claim the land for their own countries and call them "territories." This is called *colonization*. Many times, these other countries would use territories to help them fight wars. For example, Japan took hold of the Marshall Islands from the Germans during World War I. Then the United States gained military control of the islands from 1944 until 1986. The United States tested sixty-seven nuclear bombs on the islands from 1946 to 1958. In 1986, the United States agreed to pay $600 million in damages to island communities due to the effects of nuclear testing. The Republic of the Marshall Islands is now its own nation with a special association with the United States.

Edith Kanakaʻole hula dancing in Hawaiʻi

HAWAI'I

Hawai'i Statehood

Hawai'i was an independent kingdom when **Princess Lili'uokalani** was born in the city of Honolulu in 1838. She became queen in 1891, but in 1893, American sugar planters, with the help of American soldiers, removed her as queen, and the islands became the Republic of Hawai'i. In 1893, the United States made Hawai'i a territory to help them during the Spanish-American War. For the next sixty years, the political leaders in the United States and Hawai'i struggled over whether Hawai'i should officially become an American state. Some politicians did not want Hawai'i to be a state because they didn't like its multiethnic population, which included Native Hawaiians and other Pacific Islanders, as well as Filipino, Chinese, Korean, and Japanese residents. Others thought this population's ties to the Far East would be helpful in other wars. Finally, in 1959, Congress and the islands voted to make Hawai'i the fiftieth state.

POPULATION FACT

Among the Pacific Islander population, almost sixty-two thousand people identify as being Native Hawaiian in the United States, followed by Samoan and Chamorro or CHamoru. Chamorro/ CHamoru refers to the people of Guam.

Queen Lili'uokalani

WHERE DID THE LEI COME FROM?

Polynesian wayfinders brought the custom of gifting leis as symbols of both peace and friendship to the islands of Hawai'i. A lei is a garland of flowers. It looks like a necklace. Early Hawaiian leis were usually made of local flowers, leaves, vines, seeds, nuts, shells, feathers, and even sometimes animal bones and teeth. Today, leis are given not only to visitors to the islands, but also to school graduates and honored loved ones at other important celebrations. While leis today are usually made of orchids, carnations, and native blossoms, crafters also create them from man-made objects, such as ribbons, candy, and even money.

The Okina, Kahakō, and Hawaiian Language

If you live in or have visited Hawai'i, you may have noticed the okina, which is often mistaken for an apostrophe, in the middle of a Hawaiian location or word. The okina is important in the written form of the Hawaiian language. The University of Hawai'i explains that the okina is "similar to the sound between the syllables of 'oh-oh.'" Over time, the state government has recognized the importance of preserving the okina and now it is used more frequently on the islands.

Another Hawaiian pronunciation mark is the kahakō. Also referred to as a macron, the kahakō is a line above a vowel, which lengthens its sound.

' okina   **¯ kahakō**

AAPI HEROES IN SPORTS

Jeremy Lin

For two months in 2012, National Basketball Association (NBA) fans were awed by a Taiwanese American player on the New York Knicks: Jeremy Lin (1988–). While the professional basketball league had stars like the 7'6" center from China, Yao Ming, there never had been a player like Jeremy—an Asian American with a slim 6'3" frame who was dominating the game. He was so rare in the league that at first, security guards and even fellow players doubted he was on the team. Then on February 6, 2012, he came off the bench to score 25 points in a win against the then–New Jersey Nets. As the Knicks had been losing games, both Jeremy's performance and the team's win had been a complete surprise. The Knicks' coach continued to give Jeremy a lot of playing time, leading to a seven-game win streak in which Jeremy averaged over 24 points and 9 assists per game. His time played became known as "Linsanity."

Vicki Manalo Draves

Sammy Lee and Vicki Manalo Draves

Two divers were the first Asian Americans to win Olympic gold medals in 1948. Korean American Sammy Lee (1920–2016) and Filipina American Vicki Manalo Draves (1924–2010) were already friends who had both faced racial discrimination. Los Angeles–born Sammy and San Francisco native Vicki could only swim in public pools on the "international day" reserved for people of color and the day before the pools would be drained and cleaned. However, those restrictions did not stop both athletes from pursuing their passion for the high dive. Sammy even practiced diving into a sandpit. And after Sammy saw Vicki's skills at a national competition, he introduced her to a new coach, Lyle Draves, who later became Vicki's husband. (At the wedding, Sammy served as best man.) At the 1948 London Olympics, Vicki won the gold in the women's three-meter springboard before Sammy did the same in the men's ten-meter platform. Sammy, who became a doctor with the US Army Medical Corps during the Korean War, was granted a military leave to represent the United States in the 1952 Helsinki Olympics and won another gold medal in the same event.

Carissa Moore

Carissa Moore (1992–), who was born in Honolulu, Hawai'i, became the first woman to win a gold medal in the first-ever surfing event in the Olympics in 2021. She was the only Native Hawaiian member of the US team. Carissa began surfing at age five, and in ten years, was competing with world champions. She went professional in 2010, qualifying for the World Surf League's Championship Tour, which requires 150 days of international travel in a single year. At age eighteen, Carissa became the youngest person to win a surfing world title, and three years later, she was

Suni Lee

inducted into the Surfers' Hall of Fame. She created a nonprofit to encourage women's empowerment, Moore Aloha.

Sunisa "Suni" Lee

Two days before Sunisa "Suni" Lee (2003–), the first Hmong American Olympian, was to compete in the US National Gymnastics Championships, she learned that the man who helped raise her had become paralyzed from the chest down because of a tree-trimming accident in their neighborhood in St. Paul, Minnesota. Suni was going to withdraw from the 2016 competition, but John Lee, her mother's partner, whose surname Suni had taken, insisted that she continue to compete. She won gold on the uneven bars and finished second in the all-around competition. The 2020 Tokyo Summer Olympics also proved to be challenging for Suni. First, the games

were delayed until 2021 because of the pandemic. Suni broke her foot at practice during the quarantine. Her aunt and uncle died of COVID-19. Once in Tokyo, American standout Simone Biles pulled out of the Olympic gymnastics team because of mental health issues. Yet Suni persevered, winning a gold in the all-around, a silver in the team competition, and a bronze in the uneven bars.

Kristi Yamaguchi

Northern California–born Japanese American Kristi Yamaguchi (1971–) fell in love with ice skating at a young age and became an elite skater. After graduating from high school, she moved to Alberta, Canada, to train for the 1992 Olympic Games in Albertville, France. At the games, she skated a near perfect singles program, earning her and the United

States a much-wanted gold medal. She was inducted into the US Figure Skating Hall of Fame in 1998 and the World Figure Skating Hall of Fame the following year.

Chloe Kim

Southern California–born Korean American Chloe Kim (2000–) started snowboarding in local mountains at the age of four with her father. She started competing at age six as a member of a team in the mountains overlooking Los Angeles before going to Switzerland for more training for two years. She returned to California's Mammoth Mountain to continue improving her snowboarding skills and technique and began competing at a pro level at age twelve. She was homeschooled by her parents, both South Korean immigrants. The 2018 Olympic Winter Games in PyeongChang, South Korea, thrust Chloe into the public eye. She won a gold medal in the snowboarding half-pipe competition at age seventeen. Celebrated for her skills and bubbly personality (her "I'm getting hangry" tweet before her performance went viral), Chloe was riding high until she saw an insulting Instagram message about her. That degrading message, plus breaking her ankle in 2019, caused her to rethink her priorities, and she chose to take a brief break from competition to attend Princeton University, her dream school. COVID-19 derailed her academic experience, and she returned to training. At the 2022 Olympic Winter Games in Beijing, she won gold in the half-pipe for the second time.

Michael Chang

Chinese American Michael Chang (1972–) broke a number of US tennis records shortly after entering the professional tennis world at age fifteen. In 1987, he became the youngest player to win a match at the US Open and the youngest to win the US Junior National Championship. In 1988, he was the youngest to play on Centre Court at Wimbledon in sixty years, and then in 1989, he was the youngest to play on a US Davis Cup team in sixty-one years. But he secured his place in tennis history when at age seventeen, he won the French Open in Paris, the first US men's player to win on those clay courts in thirty-four years. Even more impressively, he was also the youngest man to win a Grand Slam singles title. Michael attributes his early success to his mental strength. A devoted Christian, Michael has worked closely with his family, including his Chinese immigrant parents, to steer his tennis career and their family foundation. Michael currently coaches a new crop of world-class tennis competitors, such as Japan's Kei Nishikori.

Michael Chang

MORE SPORTS HEROES

WAT MISAKA (1923–2019)
The first non-white athlete and Japanese American to be drafted by an American professional basketball team (New York Knicks)

KIM NG (1968–)
The first woman and Chinese American to serve as the general manager of a Major League Baseball team (Miami Marlins)

ERIK SPOELSTRA (1970–)
The first NBA coach of Filipino descent (Miami Heat)

RAYMOND TOWNSEND (1965–)
The first Filipino to play in the NBA (Golden State Warriors)

SAMOAN FOOTBALL PLAYERS

The number of Samoans in the United States and American Sāmoa is small, but a large percentage of Samoan boys and young men play football in American universities and even the National Football League. Football, which appeals to the Samoan fighting spirit, was introduced in high schools that the US government built in American Sāmoa in the 1960s. Young men feel they can pursue a better economic future with football. Mike Iupati, Marcus Mariota, Troy Polamalu, Junior Seau, and Tua Tagovailoa are some famous Samoan football players.

Troy Polamalu and Junior Seau

JAPANESE PROFESSIONAL BASEBALL PLAYERS

· ·

There have been a number of Asian American players in Major League Baseball ever since Filipino American Bobby Balcena of San Pedro, California, made it to the Big Leagues in 1956. However, the American public is more familiar with players who come from Asia, specifically Japan.

The long relationship between the United States and Japan in the sport began with Babe Ruth's participation in an exhibition tour in Japan in 1934. One famous Japanese baseball player in the twenty-first century is Shohei Ohtani of the Los Angeles Angels. In 2021, he was the first player in MLB history to be an All-Star as both a pitcher and hitter. Hideo Nomo of the Los Angeles Dodgers and his tornado style of pitching excited fans so much that he created "Nomo-mania" in 2002. Around the same time, another Japanese player, Ichiro Suzuki, a right fielder, was making his mark as a hitter for the Seattle Mariners. Ichiro finished his career with the most hits, 4,367, by a high-level professional baseball player.

Shohei Ohtani

Dat Nguyen

His mother was pregnant with Dat Nguyen (1975–) when Dat's mother, father, and his five siblings fled in a shrimp boat from South Vietnam before North Vietnamese military forces took over Saigon in 1975. Dat was born in September that year in a refugee camp in Fort Chaffee, Arkansas. The large family moved to a small coastal town in Texas, where Dat excelled in football in high school despite being taunted for being Asian. He was good enough to be offered a scholarship to Texas A&M University, becoming the first Vietnamese American football player in the school's history. Dat was 5'11", which is considered small for a linebacker. But he averaged 11.3 tackles a game to become the career leading tackler for Texas A&M and was recognized as one of college football's top linebackers. A third-round draft pick by the Dallas Cowboys, he was the first person of Vietnamese descent to play in the National Football League. After retiring from the game, Dat has served as a coach and a sports broadcaster.

Tiger Woods

When a golfer wins the Masters Tournament in Augusta, Georgia, he puts on the winner's green jacket, a tradition of the storied Augusta National Golf Club. In 1997, a twenty-one-year-old Tiger Woods (1975–) of Cypress, California, became the youngest man to wear the green jacket in a record-breaking win that made him a huge star in a game that was dominated by white players. Tiger is of Black and Asian descent. He playfully referred to himself as a Cabalasian (Caucasian/Black/Asian). His father, Earl, had been a US Army officer when he met Tiger's mother, Kultida, in Bangkok, Thailand, in 1969. Tiger was born six years later in Southern California. Tiger became a golfing sensation, winning a record-tying ninety-two PGA Tour events and fifteen major championships. His competitiveness and clothing style gave the game of golf a new, cool image. He wears his trademark bright red shirt on advice from his mother, who says that it is his power color.

Tiger Woods

BUILDING AND GROWING AMERICA

WHY COME TO AMERICA?

Many Asian people came to America due to political and economic problems in their home countries. For the early Chinese, it was the Taiping Rebellion in the mid-1800s that took 20 million lives. Some peasants in the countryside were poor and were drawn to stories of finding gold in parts of California. Some Japanese men wanted to flee their country so they didn't have to fight in the Russo-Japanese War. As eldest brothers usually inherited all the wealth, second and third brothers left to work on sugar plantations in Hawai'i or farms on the Pacific West Coast. People from the island of Okinawa, which became part of Japan in 1879, had to pay a lot of taxes, so many Okinawans left for Hawai'i and Latin America. Poor or struggling families often released their daughters to get married to men in America, hoping that their future would be improved in a new land. Koreans who wanted to escape harsh Japanese military rule moved to the United States. After World War II, Korea was split into two zones—the North, occupied by the Soviet Union, and the South, by the United States. Some North Koreans fled to the South during the Korean War and later made their way to the United States.

A Chinese immigrant family arriving on the West Coast

WORKING IN THE UNITED STATES

From their first presence in the United States, Asian immigrants have contributed to the economic growth of this nation. Chinese laborers built the railroad routes throughout the United States, sometimes losing their lives in the process. Approximately eleven thousand Chinese immigrants worked on the Transcontinental Railroad that stretched from the East Coast of the United States to the West Coast. They also worked in the gold mines and then turned to farming, cooking, and washing clothes for a living.

Filipinos were the first to establish an ethnic community in the United States. They worked in the shrimping industry in the Louisiana bayou from 1760. More than two hundred years later, Vietnamese refugees would continue the work of shrimpers in the same area. Young Filipino men and Japanese immigrants worked on farms in the fields of California in the 1900s. They replaced Chinese workers, who were not allowed to come to the United States after 1882. Many of these Japanese agricultural workers later ran successful farms all throughout the Pacific West Coast, only to lose their businesses when they were forcibly removed under a presidential order during World War II in 1942.

ROAD TO CITIZENSHIP

The Naturalization Act of 1790 prevented almost all Asian immigrants from becoming naturalized US citizens until the mid-twentieth century. Here's a timeline of when citizenship rights were finally granted to certain ethnicities.

- **1943:** Chinese (Magnuson Act)

- **1946:** Filipinos and Indians (Luce-Celler Act)

- **1952:** Japanese and Koreans (McCarran-Walter Act)

Chinese workers on the Transcontinental Railroad

EARLY FOOD PIONEERS

Ho "Charles" Kim

Ho "Charles" Kim (1884–1968) and his partner, **Hyung-soon "Harry" Kim**, were pioneering Korean immigrant farmers in California's Central Valley. Koreans first came to America to work on plantations in Hawai'i or in service-type industries on the mainland. Charles, who arrived in 1914, formed the Kim Brothers agricultural company with Harry. While many farmers declared bankruptcy during the Great Depression of 1929, the two Kims kept working and created new varieties of peaches and nectarines. Their fuzzless nectarines, known as the "Le Grand" and "Sun Grand" varieties, are still grown today.

Lue Gim Gong

Lue Gim Gong (1857–1925), who was known as a citrus wizard, left his village in China for the United States at the age of fifteen in 1872. After he became sick with tuberculosis in the Massachusetts cold, he returned to China for a short time before deciding that he wanted to live in America. At the time, the Chinese Exclusion Act of 1882 was part of US law. Lue had to enter the country by saying he had a business awaiting him in Massachusetts. Instead, he headed for the warmth of Florida and worked in the orange groves. Even though there were laws that didn't allow Asians to become US citizens, Lue, through the help of some important friends, was able to become a US citizen in 1877. While in DeLand, Central Florida, Lue began experimenting with growing fruits that could tolerate cold weather. That led to the creation of a new, sweet orange named Lue Gim Gong, an orange that could grow in cold weather and become ripe in early fall. This helped the Florida citrus industry grow and sell even more oranges.

FIRST GENERATION

There are different names for immigrants and the first generation born in the United States. Japanese Americans call the ones who first came to America the first generation. Others call the first ones to be born in the United States the first generation.

Lue Gim Gong harvesting oranges in DeLand, Central Florida

Tsuru Yamauchi

Tsuru Yamauchi (1890–1990) was born and raised in Okinawa, a small island west of Japan's main island. One of twelve children (although five died at a young age), Tsuru didn't go to school and instead helped her family by sewing. When she was thirteen, she learned how to make tofu from dried soybeans. After grinding soaked beans by hand early in the morning, she sold blocks of tofu as a sidewalk vendor. She left for Hawai'i at age twenty to become a picture bride. A picture bride was a Japanese woman who exchanged photos with Japanese men in Hawai'i and the West Coast of America before crossing the Pacific Ocean to get married. After giving birth to five children, Tsuru and her husband bought a tofu shop in Honolulu. They continued making tofu during World War II. The family business expanded to Los Angeles before being bought by a larger company, Japan-based House Foods, which now manufactures tofu in Orange County, California.

Tsuru Yamauchi making tofu from soybeans

WHAT DO WE CALL OURSELVES?

These are some common terms that Asian Americans use to describe themselves.

1. 1.5 (one point five): Asian Americans who came to the United States as children

2. ABC, which stands for American Born Chinese: a phrase used by some Chinese Americans

3. CHamoru: people of Guam

4. Desi: a person or family who come from India, Pakistan, or Bangladesh and live in another country like the United States

5. Filipino: a person of Philippine origin or descent who lives in the United States (Filipinx is another option, or Filipina, which is used specifically for women)

6. Hapa haole (Hawaiian): a person of white and Native Hawaiian descent

7. Issei: a first-generation Japanese American, first Japanese to come to America

8. Kama'āina: a person who has lived in Hawai'i for a long time who is not Native Hawaiian

9. Kānaka maoli: Native Hawaiians

10. Khmer: main ethnic group within the nation of Cambodia

11. Nisei: a second-generation Japanese American, the children of the Issei

12. Sansei: a third-generation Japanese American, the children of the Nisei

US IMMIGRATION LAWS

Since the time the Chinese first entered the United States, politicians have tried to exclude them, other Asian immigrants, and Pacific Islanders from making America their permanent home. An exclusion is when you leave someone or something out. These groups were discriminated against because they were different from European immigrants. They spoke different languages, looked different, and sometimes followed different religions and traditions.

But these same people worked and contributed to the United States, fought in the army and navy, and made the country a better place. Over time, they put pressure on the government to change these laws of exclusion. There has been much progress, but there are still exclusions, especially those that affect Pacific Islanders.

Chinese Exclusion Act

In 1882, US president Chester A. Arthur signed a law to stop the immigration of Chinese laborers for ten years and not allow any Chinese people to become US citizens. This was the first time a major US law restricted immigration and the first time a specific ethnic group was named in such an exclusion. While Chinese newcomers could still visit and conduct business, they were completely banned from moving to America in 1902. Immigration was not reopened until the Magnuson Act passed during World War II in 1943. The Magnuson Act repealed the Chinese Exclusion Act of 1882, allowing Chinese people to finally become naturalized citizens. It also allowed for Chinese immigration to the United States, but only 105 people could arrive every year.

A Japanese picture bride

Gentlemen's Agreement

While Chinese individuals were being excluded from moving to America, Japanese laborers were still able to come in because of an 1894 treaty between the United States and Japan. As more Japanese immigrated to the United States, especially to California, they began to face more discrimination. Discrimination is when a group of people is treated differently because of who they are or how they look. The city of San Francisco decided that Japanese and Korean students should be sent to different schools than white students. Chinese students were already being sent to different schools. The Japanese government became upset and from 1906 to 1907, negotiated with President Theodore Roosevelt to come to a compromise, which was called the Gentlemen's Agreement. Under this agreement, San Francisco would stop sending Japanese students to different schools and the Japanese government would not issue passports to new workers seeking to go to America. The United States would allow Japanese people with family already in America to immigrate. Many Japanese women became "picture brides," women who sent their pictures to Japanese men already in America, who would then agree to marry them without ever meeting them. After the marriage was filed in Japan, the women would be allowed to come to the United States. This helped the Japanese immigrant community in the United States grow.

Immigration Act of 1924

This law stopped nearly all immigration from Japan to the United States. It also greatly reduced the number of newcomers from southern and eastern Europe. While 30,842 Japanese immigrated to the United States in 1907, only 3,503 were able to move to America between 1931 and 1950.

Tydings-McDuffie Act of 1934

In 1934, President Franklin D. Roosevelt signed a bill, also known as the Philippine Independence Act, that would grant the Philippines independence within ten years. As a commonwealth government, the Philippines would remain a US territory, but anything related to war and money would be controlled by the Philippine people. This meant Filipinos were now considered not Americans and would be excluded from coming to the United States because of the same exclusion acts against the Chinese, Japanese, Koreans, and other Asians.

Immigration Act of 1952

This law, also called the McCarran-Walter Act, allowed a small number of new people to arrive from Asia. Some Japanese and Korean people who had been living in the United States were finally able to become citizens.

Immigration and Nationality Act of 1965

In 1965, President Lyndon B. Johnson signed the bill that would change immigration in the United States for decades. The Immigration and Nationality Act of 1965 stopped exclusion laws, which made it possible for people to come to the United States no matter where they were from. This helped families who had been separated reunite and allowed refugees and workers from all over the world to come to the United States. By the 1990s, 31 percent of total immigrants in the United States were from Asia.

Lyndon B. Johnson signing the Immigration and Nationality Act of 1965

ANGEL ISLAND, SAN FRANCISCO

Angel Island is an island near the city of San Francisco that was used as an immigration station, or stopping point. From 1910 to 1940, around 300,000 to 500,000 immigrants—100,000 of them Chinese—from eighty countries had to go through Angel Island. During that period, Chinese immigrants were forced to stay on the island for the longest time. Most of the Chinese immigrants were forced to stay for two to three weeks, while some were forced to stay for months under terrible conditions. They carved poems of despair in the wooden walls of the immigration center that held them. More than two hundred poems written in Chinese were discovered underneath paint and have been preserved at Angel Island State Park.

Immigrants arriving on Angel Island

NOTABLE LANDMARKS IN HISTORIC ETHNIC TOWNS

Many cities in the United States have neighborhoods where people from a specific ancestry settled a long time ago. These neighborhoods are full of wonderful stories and reminders of the sacrifices made by the first generation to come to America.

Chinatowns

CASTELAR ELEMENTARY SCHOOL
in Los Angeles, California

. . . .

This is the second-oldest school in Los Angeles. It is located in the center of present-day Chinatown and has a Mandarin Chinese language immersion program.

DRAGON'S GATE
in San Francisco, California

. . . .

Chinese American architect **Clayton Lee** designed this gate when he was twenty-seven. The south-facing gate was completed in 1970.

HISTORIC DOYERS STREET
in New York, New York

. . . .

This street has a sharp bend in the middle where a mural of Chinese American photographer **Corky Lee** is painted on a wall.

PUI TAK CENTER
in Chicago, Illinois

. . . .

This building is Chicago Chinatown's only historical landmark. It used to be the majestic On Leong Merchants Association Building, which was constructed from 1926 to 1928.

Dragon's Gate in San Francisco, Calilfornia

Lan Su Chinese Garden in Portland, Oregon

CHINATOWN GATE
in Boston, Massachusetts

· ·

Two guardian lions greet visitors in a gift from the Taiwanese government in 1982.

WO FAT
RESTAURANT BUILDING
in Honolulu, Hawai'i

· ·

Representing Chinatown's long history in O'ahu dating back to the mid-1800s, this iconic building was built for Wo Fat Restaurant in 1938 after earlier buildings were destroyed in fires.

LAN SU CHINESE GARDEN
in Portland, Oregon

· ·

Craftspeople from Portland's sister city in China, Suzhou, came in 1999 to build this city-block-long garden designed in the style of China's Ming dynasty (1368–1644).

Japantowns

NOGUCHI PLAZA
in Los Angeles, California

. . . .

This 1983 sculpture has two twelve-foot-long columns and is outside Little Tokyo's Japanese American Cultural and Community Center. The sculpture was dedicated to the Issei by designer **Isamu Noguchi**.

ORIGAMI FOUNTAINS
in San Francisco, California

. . . .

Sculptor **Ruth Asawa** created twin origami-style lotus blossoms in fountains in 1974.

SAN JOSE BUDDHIST TEMPLE
in San Jose, California

. . . .

Two Japanese immigrant woodworkers, **Shinzaburo Nishiura** and **Gentaro Nishiura**, completed this grand temple designed by **George Gentoku Shimamoto** in 1937.

Little Indias

GOVINDA TEMPLE
in Jersey City, New Jersey

. . . .

Located in a simple storefront building, this temple serves one thousand Hindu households who have roots in the western Indian state of Gujarat.

Origami Fountains in San Francisco, California

Koreatowns

BROWN DERBY PLAZA
in Los Angeles, California

· ·

This hat-shaped dome was part of the first Brown Derby Restaurant, which opened in 1926. It was later moved to a shopping center in the middle of present-day Koreatown.

Brown Derby Plaza in Los Angeles, California

Historic Filipinotown

FILIPINO AMERICAN WWII VETERANS MEMORIAL
in Los Angeles, California

· ·

This is the first monument dedicated to Filipino and Filipino American soldiers who fought for the United States in World War II. It was finished in 2006.

Little Saigon

PHUOC LOC THO
in Orange County, California

· ·

This garden is a kind of town square for the Vietnamese American community in Orange County, California. It was built in 1987.

Cambodia Town

MURALS ON ANAHEIM STREET
in Long Beach, California

· ·

Anaheim Street is near the Pacific Ocean and is full of colorful murals celebrating the strength of the Cambodian people, whose population in Long Beach is the largest in the nation.

Thai Town

KINNARA MONUMENTS
in Hollywood, California

· ·

Two statues of kinnara, which are half-human, half-lion mythical figures, were brought from Thailand to the United States in a 2013 project. The kinnara stand on seventeen-foot-high lampposts overlooking the first official Thai district in the United States.

Thai Town Kinnara Monuments in Hollywood, California

AAPI HEROES IN ARCHITECTURE AND DESIGN

I.M. Pei with the Louvre Pyramid in Paris, France

I.M. Pei

I.M. Pei (1917–2019), one of the most notable architects in the world, was born Ieoh Ming Pei in Canton (now Guangzhou), China. The son of a successful banker, he moved with his family for his father's work in Hong Kong and then Shanghai.

In Shanghai, I.M. became immediately mesmerized by the architecture as he watched a twenty-five-story hotel being built. He studied architecture at both MIT and the Harvard Graduate School of Design and was hired by commercial real estate developer William Zeckendorf to

oversee the design of high-rise buildings in Manhattan. By 1960, I.M. had launched his own company, which, at its height, employed three hundred people. His projects included museums, concert halls, hospitals, office towers, and civic buildings. I.M. is probably best known for creating

Maya Lin with the Vietnam Memorial in Washington, DC

the iconic glass pyramid that serves as an entry to the Louvre, the famed art museum in Paris. His other notable works include the East Building of the National Gallery of Art, the John F. Kennedy Library, the John Hancock Tower, the Jacob Javits Convention Center, and the Rock & Roll Hall of Fame and Museum in Cleveland. I.M.'s modern style is defined by strong, clean lines with a focus on simplicity and geometric shape. He received the highest honors in his field, including the Gold Medal of the American Institute of Architects and the Pritzker Prize. Although he did not return to his birthplace in China until 1974, he was proud of his heritage and gave his children Chinese names.

Maya Lin
Maya Lin (1959–) was a senior at Yale University when she submitted the winning

design in a national competition for the Vietnam Veterans Memorial to be built in Washington, DC. The memorial's simple presentation of 58,318 names of soldiers engraved on a wall received worldwide attention. It helped create a new way of memorializing tragic events. Maya, the daughter of Chinese immigrant scholars in Ohio, explores the theme of landscapes in her art and the architectural projects she creates in her New York City studio. A 1996 documentary about her, *Maya Lin: A Strong Clear Vision*, won an Academy Award for best documentary. In 2016, President Barack Obama awarded Maya the Presidential Medal of Freedom.

Isamu Noguchi

Isamu Noguchi (1904–1988) was a mixed-race Japanese American sculptor, landscape architect, and designer of modern furniture. He became well known for creating light structures made of bamboo and Japanese paper. His Japanese father was a poet, while his mother, a white American woman, was a writer and editor. Born in Los Angeles, he spent his childhood with his mother in various locations in Japan. While in training to become an artist, he lived in France, China, Japan, and finally New York City, where he opened his own studio in Long Island City. He created sculptures, installations, and murals in Paris, Miami, Mexico City, Seattle, and Los Angeles's Little Tokyo. His former art studio is now a museum of his artwork.

Isamu Noguchi with a model of the Black Sun statue in Seattle

Vera Wang with a bridal dress collection

Vera Wang

Vera Wang (1949–) is one of the most famous fashion designers in the world. She is known for her wedding dresses and one-of-a-kind dresses for celebrities of all ages. Vera, a native New Yorker, is the daughter of a Chinese immigrant who helped to build a successful oil refining, trading, and pharmaceutical company doing business in Asia. After working as a fashion editor for Condé Nast and Vogue magazines, Vera moved into designing. When she was planning for her wedding at the age of forty, she couldn't find many modern bridal dresses. She decided to open her own bridal boutique. Her successful brand now includes perfumes, eyeglasses, and jewelry.

RACIAL DISCRIMINATION

EARLY CHALLENGES

California's gold rush in the mid-1800s brought thousands of people to the West Coast, including approximately twenty thousand from China. These Chinese travelers made up more than 20 percent of the mining workforce. They were the largest group of non-white workers searching for gold.

Chinese workers faced racial discrimination in the United States. They were taxed for being foreigners and, as the gold rush slowed down, they were banned from other jobs. Some Asian workers were even killed, most tragically in the Chinese Massacre of 1871 when a mob of over five hundred people in Los Angeles killed eighteen Chinese men. In 1882, President Chester A. Arthur signed the first Chinese Exclusion Act, which limited all Chinese immigration until the law was repealed during World War II.

FIGHTING BACK

Lee Yick

During this time of high anti-Asian discrimination, a Chinese laundryman in San Francisco named Lee Yick fought back. For over twenty years, he owned Yick Wo, one of 240 laundries owned and operated by Chinese immigrants in San Francisco. In 1885, the board of supervisors denied the license renewals of nearly two hundred Chinese laundries, including Yick Wo. Lee, feeling that he and his countrymen were being unfairly discriminated against, defied the board and continued to operate his laundry. After he was found in violation of an 1880 ordinance, he was arrested, fined, and imprisoned in the county jail.

Lee took his case to the California Supreme Court and won. The judges decided the laundry ordinance violated the Fourth Amendment, which grants every person in the US equal

Lee Yick

Bhagat Singh Thind

protection under the law. The May 10, 1886, decision in *Yick Wo v. Sheriff Hopkins* is a landmark legal case that is still cited today.

Bhagat Singh Thind

South Asians were also heavily discriminated against at this time. They were called the "least desirable race" by the 1911 US Immigration Commission. Bhagat Singh Thind (1892–1967) came to Seattle in 1913 from his birthplace in a region of India where many Sikhs tried to escape control by British colonial authorities. As a Sikh, Bhagat wore a turban as part of his religious practice. When the United States entered World War I in 1917, he enlisted in the US Army and was the first serviceman to be allowed to wear a turban with his official uniform.

While in the military, Bhagat applied for US citizenship. The courts went back and forth on whether to approve his naturalization.

The Naturalization Act of 1790 ordered that only "free white person(s) of good character" could become citizens. Bhagat argued that he should be considered a white man, but the Bureau of Naturalization disagreed. The case went to the Supreme Court, which unanimously ruled in 1923 that Indians like Bhagat (incorrectly referred to as Hindus) could not be considered white. As a result, dozens of naturalized Americans from India lost their citizenship. Bhagat was finally able to become a US citizen in 1935, when Congress extended naturalization rights to all World War I veterans. Most other Indian immigrants would have to wait to become citizens until the laws changed in 1946.

Mitsuye Endo

On February 19, 1942, President Franklin D. Roosevelt signed Executive Order 9066. A

few months earlier, the Japanese military had bombed Pearl Harbor in Hawaiʻi. The American government said they were worried that anyone with a Japanese background would side with Japan in World War II. But that was not the case. This order forced Japanese Americans to leave their homes on the West Coast. More than 120,000 of them were imprisoned in ten American concentration camps. Two-thirds of those held in the camps were Nisei (second generation) who were born in the US. Most of them had never even stepped foot in Japan.

Four Nisei legally challenged the order and were arrested on suspicion of being national security risks. Only one of the plaintiffs—the only woman, Mitsuye Endo (1920–2006)— received a favorable Supreme Court ruling, which led to the closure of the concentration camps and the return of Japanese Americans to the West Coast in 1945. Four decades later, the courts ruled that they were wrong in their decision against the three Nisei men. The courts said the United States had hidden military documents stating the men were not dangerous and had lied when they claimed the men were national security risks. No Issei or Nisei in the United States was charged with spying during World War II.

Esther Takei Nishio

Esther Takei Nishio (1925–2019), a Nisei, had lived in Venice, California, before she and her family were sent to the Granada concentration camp in Amache, Colorado. In the summer of 1944, she was recruited by a new organization based in Pasadena, California, called Friends of the American Way, which worked to return Japanese Americans to Southern California. Nineteen-year-old Esther served as a test case as the first Japanese American not in a special category to be allowed back on the West Coast. While many in Pasadena welcomed her, others didn't, leading to harassment of her and her host family. American veterans came to her defense and eventually the bullying stopped.

Segregated Schools for Chinese in San Francisco

For decades, children of Chinese descent could not be educated in the same classrooms as white students in San Francisco school systems. Chinese parents sued, and in 1885, the California Supreme Court agreed that public education had to be open to all children. However, instead of allowing Chinese students into white classrooms, an all-Chinese school, considered to provide separate but equal educational opportunities, was opened. Over time, with fewer Chinese allowed into California because of exclusion laws, less money was available to finance these segregated schools. These all-Chinese institutions were mostly gone by the 1930s. School desegregation was largely attained through financial concerns rather than constitutional ones.

Esther Takei Nishio in Pasadena, California

Anti-Miscegenation Laws

In states like California, local governments passed anti-miscegenation laws, which banned ethnic minorities from marrying white people. These laws affected thousands of people who had traveled from the Philippines, a US colony from 1898 to 1946, to fill low-wage jobs. These Filipino workers were called manongs, a term for a beloved older brother or relative.

Many manongs remained single their whole lives. California's anti-miscegenation law was finally repealed in 1948. *Loving v. Virginia* was a landmark case in which interracial marriage was finally legalized for the whole nation in 1967. Today, three in ten Asian immigrant newlyweds marry outside of their race and ethnicity. For US-born Asian Americans, the number is greater: 46 percent, or almost half.

KKK in Galveston Bay

The Ku Klux Klan, or KKK, is a hate group in the United States that targets non-whites. In 1981, they burned two Vietnamese shrimp boats in Galveston, Texas. The Vietnamese immigrants challenged these racist threats to their livelihood and future by filing a lawsuit against the Knights of the KKK. A judge issued a court order to end the harassment and shut down white nationalist

Angela Oh working with others to achieve social justice

training camps. By not backing down, the Vietnamese American community has been able to thrive in Texas. Today, more than eighty thousand live in nearby Houston.

TROUBLE IN LOS ANGELES

Los Angeles was on fire on April 29, 1992—both literally and politically. The acquittal of four Los Angeles Police Department officers in the videotaped beating of Rodney King, an unarmed Black man, brought on protests.

Arson, looting, vandalism, and violence erupted throughout the city. Among the targets were Korean Americans, especially immigrants who owned shops in historic Black neighborhoods. The media played a role in pushing conflict between Korean Americans and Black Americans instead of focusing on people taking action against police violence. Korean Americans refer to this tragic event as Saigu, or 4-2-9, marking the starting date of the Los Angeles riots, also referred to as the Los Angeles civil disturbance.

Angela Oh

Angela E. Oh (1955–), a second-generation Korean American and an attorney, had just become president of the Korean American Bar Association in 1992. An experienced trial lawyer, she served as the public spokesperson for the Korean American community. She was able to provide a larger story of how Korean immigrants, no matter their educational background or past professional experience, often had to rely on opening small stores in Black neighborhoods to make a living in

Southern California. In helping the public become more aware of Korean American concerns, Angela became active at the regional and national level to address issues of racial reconciliation. Now an ordained Zen Buddhist priest, she has cofounded a program that uses meditation to bring healing to people seeking to achieve social justice.

COVID-19

Asian Americans became the unfortunate scapegoats of the COVID-19 pandemic, as even the president of the United States used inflammatory language like "China virus" and "Kung flu" in national addresses. As a result, many people of Asian ancestry from metropolitan areas like San Francisco and New York City to small towns with small Asian populations became targets of both harassment and hate crimes. An ethnic studies professor at San Francisco State University, **Russell Jeung** (1962–), could not stand back passively. His Asian American Studies department, Chinese for Affirmative Action, and the Asian Pacific Policy and Planning Council joined together to collect data of anti-Asian and anti–Pacific Islander hate crimes. From March 19, 2020, to March 31, 2022, their project, Stop AAPI Hate, gathered reports of almost 11,500 hate incidents throughout the country. This information helped make activists, the media, and politicians aware of these incidents and to fight against them.

SERVICE OF FILIPINO NURSES IN THE UNITED STATES

Throughout the history of the United States, Filipino nurses have come from their island home to fill the gaps in American health care. Because of colonization, Western nursing schools and medical facilities were created in the Philippines in the early 1900s. Immigration laws were changed to allow more trained Filipino nurses to both work and live in the United States. During the HIV/AIDS epidemic in the 1980s, Filipino nurses came to serve patients with AIDS, who some health practitioners refused to treat. From 1980 to 1990, the population of Filipino Americans rose from approximately 775,000 to 1,400,000. During the COVID-19 pandemic, 24 percent of nurses who died from complications of the coronavirus were Filipino. Only 4 percent of the total registered nurses in the US are of Filipino descent.

Some immigrant nurses are taken advantage of in America. In 2019, two hundred Filipino nurses sued and won a case against a New York–based nursing home company that threatened them with non-payment if they quit due to bad working conditions. The case was settled in 2022, with the nursing home paying the nurses $3 million.

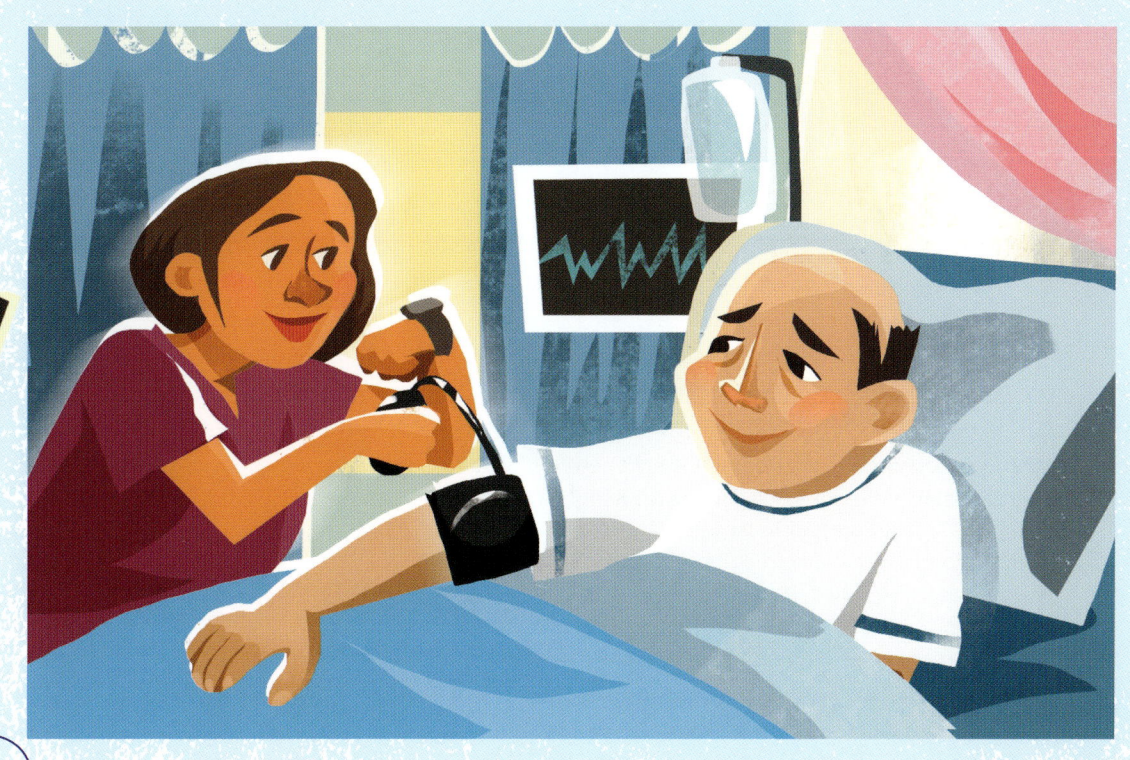

AAPI HEROES IN ACTIVISM

Grace Lee Boggs

Ever since she was young, Chinese American Grace Lee Boggs (1915–2015) was a thinker, drawn to the big issues of life. She was the daughter of a Chinese restaurant owner and lived around mostly white neighbors in Jackson Heights, New York. She was often asked where she was from by people assuming that she couldn't possibly be American. When she moved to Chicago, Grace became active in the struggles of the Black community through a tenants-rights organization. She eventually moved to Detroit to edit a radical newsletter called *Correspondence*. There, she met and married an autoworker and Alabama-born Black activist, James Boggs. Together, they worked to deal with issues of racial inequality. She was also an author and wrote an autobiography called *Living for Change*.

Yuri Kochiyama

When Yuri Kochiyama (1921–2014), her husband, Bill, and their children moved to Harlem in 1960, she became political. Born in San Pedro, California, she had been among the 120,000 Japanese Americans removed from their homes during World War II. Her main activity during her detention in Jerome, Arkansas, was leading a letter-writing campaign to three thousand Nisei soldiers who served overseas. She met Bill, a soldier with the 100th/442nd Regimental Combat Team (see page 50), at an event in Jerome. The couple moved to New York City, Bill's hometown, in 1946. In Harlem, the couple became involved with the Harlem Parent Committee and fought

Grace Lee Boggs

Haunani-Kay Trask

for better education for inner-city children. Yuri was arrested for the first time in a civil protest to demand the hiring of Black and Puerto Rican workers at a construction site. During the 1960s, she became friends with Black civil rights leader Malcolm X, who visited the Kochiyama household to meet a group of atomic bomb survivors from Japan. Yuri saw Malcolm X's shocking assassination at his talk at the Audubon Ballroom in 1965 and was even captured in a photo of her cradling his head onstage. She was not identified in those photos. Yuri became one of the most beloved Asian American activists of the twentieth century.

Haunani-Kay Trask

Haunani-Kay Trask (1949–2021) fought for Native Hawaiians (kānaka maoli) like herself to have more say in determining the future of their people in Hawai'i. In 1993, the hundredth anniversary of the overthrow of Queen Lili'uokalani, she, other kānaka maoli leaders, and fifteen thousand people marched on 'Iolani Palace in Honolulu to demand the return of native lands held in trust by the state. She wanted the government to allow the kānaka maoli to control their own territory, but the Hawai'i Legislature rejected such proposals. Though born in San Francisco, Haunani-Kay grew up on O'ahu with her five siblings and attended Kamehameha School in Honolulu, dedicated to educating kānaka maoli children. She earned both her bachelor's degree and doctorate in political science

Lydia X. Z. Brown

from the University of Wisconsin at Madison before returning to the islands to teach at the University of Hawai'i at Manoa, where she founded the Kamakakuokalani Center for Hawaiian Studies. A groundbreaking writer of both political work and poetry, Haunani-Kay retired in 2010. After her death from cancer at age seventy-one, her former faculty colleagues raised $200,000 to write a biography of her life and about the kānaka maoli political movements in the twentieth and twenty-first centuries.

Lydia X. Z. Brown

Lydia X. Z. Brown (1993–) was born in China and adopted by an American family at the age of one. Identified as having autism in the eighth grade, Lydia was told to be quiet about their diagnosis. However, they instead decided to advocate for people with disabilities through organizations like the Boston chapter of the Autistic Self Advocacy Network. For their early achievements, Lydia was honored by President Barack Obama at the White House in 2013. Lydia earned a law degree and, as an attorney, now fights for rights for people with disabilities.

MORE ACTIVIST HEROES

PHILIP VERA CRUZ (1904–1994)
Vice president of the Farm Workers of America union in California in the 1960s, becoming the highest ranking Filipino American in that union

K. W. LEE (1928–)
The first Asian and Korean immigrant to be hired as a journalist by a US daily newspaper

DALE MINAMI (1946–)
Attorney who successfully led the legal challenge of the mass incarceration of Japanese Americans, thirty-five years after World War II

CHANNAPHA KHAMVONGSA (1973–)
Created Legacies of War, a nonprofit organization to raise awareness about bombs still buried in Laos that were hurting and killing innocent people

Siobhon Rumurang McManus

Vishavjit Singh

Vishavjit Singh (1971–) was studying epidemiology and biostatistics for advanced degrees at the University of California at Santa Barbara when he recommitted himself to following the Sikh faith. He decided to wear a turban and stop cutting his hair, two practices of Sikhism, which is the fifth-largest major religion in the world. With the rise of Islamophobia after the 9/11 attacks in New York City, Vishavjit found himself the target of attacks while he worked as a computer programmer in Connecticut. He used his skills in drawing to create cartoons with Sikh characters. After a white supremacist shot multiple innocent worshippers at a Sikh house of worship in Wisconsin in 2012, Vishavjit wore a Captain America costume with his turban and walked the streets of New York City. He spoke to strangers about what it meant to be Sikh in the twenty-first century.

Siobhon Rumurang McManus

Siobhon Rumurang McManus, a native of Guam, had graduated in 2017 with a bachelor's degree in English from Northwest University in Kirkland, just outside Seattle, Washington, when she received a call from her family in the CHamoru town of Agat. Her Palauan paternal grandmother, who had suffered multiple strokes, needed help. Siobhon, who had previously nursed her CHamoru maternal grandmother during her high school years, didn't hesitate and got on a plane to her hometown. After six months of caregiving, her grandmother died. Siobhon, again immersed in the women-based community of her island upbringing, recommitted herself to serve her people. She began teaching English at the same school she had attended. While writing poetry, she also protested the destruction of forests for a US military base. Siobhon worked with her father to open a new charter school for island students. Her work in education contributed to her being chosen as a 2020 NDN Changemaker Fellow, dedicated to improving the lives of native peoples.

FIGHTING FOR AMERICA

Asian Americans have been part of this nation's military for more than two hundred years. Historians believe that more than seventy Chinese fought either with the army or navy for both the Union and Confederacy during the US Civil War, followed by Filipinos, Pacific Islanders, Indians, and even a small number of Indonesians, Japanese, Pakistanis, and Malaysians.

WORLD WAR I AND WORLD WAR II

World War I took place between 1914 and 1918, mostly in Europe, but fighting also spread to the Middle East, Africa, and Asia. At that time, there were approximately 180,000 Asian Americans living in the United States, including 100,000 Japanese Americans, 60,000 Chinese Americans, and 5,000 Filipino Americans. Private **Tomas Mateo Claudio**, formerly a student at the University of Nevada, became the first and only Filipino American serviceman to be killed in a battle in France in 1918. A Chinese American soldier, Private **Henry Chinn**, was also killed in action in France's Argonne Forest, while his fellow Chinese American comrade in the 77th Infantry Division, **Sing Lau Kee**, went on to be awarded a Distinguished Service Cross for his heroism in running eight miles through explosions and gunfire to communicate military orders. Sing, who was elevated to sergeant from private, was the first Chinese American to receive a combat medal in United States history.

Soldiers in the Philippines were part of its own national guard during World War I. In Hawaiʻi, 838 resident Japanese were drafted into a segregated unit, Company D of the National Guard, which, like the unit in the Philippines, did not see combat. A smaller number of first-generation Japanese

Asian Americans in military uniform

Americans on the mainland joined units like the 328th Infantry Regiment, 82nd Division, and in exchange for service, were promised US citizenship in the future.

Asian Americans and Pacific Islanders were active participants in World War II military units.

More than twenty thousand Chinese American men, or one out of every five in the United States, served in the US Armed Forces. Unlike Filipino Americans and Japanese Americans, 75 percent of the Chinese American soldiers were members of non-segregated units. The Japanese American

100th/442nd Regimental Combat Team, made up of Nisei infantrymen from Hawaiʻi and people from the mass incarceration camps on the mainland, was the most decorated military unit of its size and length of service in the history of the US military.

THE KOREAN AND VIETNAM WARS

In the 1950s and 1960s, the United States became involved in wars in Korea and Vietnam. These are called the Korean War and the Vietnam War.

By the time of the Korean War in the 1950s, Asian American segregated military units no longer existed. Los Angeles–born Korean American **Young Oak Kim**, who had been a captain of the 100th/442nd Regimental Combat Team, became the first person of color to command a battalion in combat during the conflict in Korea. Of the 36,572 fatalities during the Korean War, 241 were Asian Americans and 148 were Pacific Islanders.

The thirty-five thousand Asian Americans who fought for the United States in the Vietnam War were sometimes mistaken for the enemy in their own military units and were discriminated against. While only a small number were killed in action (139 Asian Americans and 229 Pacific Islanders), many returned with PTSD (post-traumatic stress disorder) from being discriminated against on the front lines. During this time, a number of Asian American activists mobilized to protest against the war.

Young Oak Kim leading the 100th/442nd Regimental Combat Team

TIMELINE OF AMERICA'S INVOLVEMENT IN WARS IN ASIA

WORLD WAR II

- **December 1941:** President Franklin D. Roosevelt officially declares war on Japan after Japan bombs Pearl Harbor in Hawai'i.

- **August 1945:** Japan surrenders days after the atomic bombings in Hiroshima and Nagasaki.

KOREAN WAR

- **June 1950:** President Harry Truman formally orders US ground troops to defend South Korea from a North Korean invasion.

- **July 1953:** The United States, China, North Korea, and South Korea agree to an armistice to end the war.

VIETNAM WAR

- **August 1964:** Congress passes the Gulf of Tonkin Resolution, which authorizes the president to send armed forces to actively engage in the Vietnam War.

- **February and March 1965:** President Lyndon Johnson approves bombings of North Vietnam and the Ho Chi Minh trail. The first US combat troops enter South Vietnam.

- **January 1973:** President Richard Nixon signs the Paris Peace Accords, ending direct US involvement in the Vietnam War.

AAPI WAR HEROES

Felix Balderry

Felix Balderry (1842–1895) was among the very few known Filipinos to have fought for the Union Army during the Civil War. Born on Monmouth Island in the Philippines, he joined the crew of a US merchant ship when he was just a teenager. That assignment took him to Michigan, where he enlisted in Company A of the 11th Michigan Infantry. During some furious battles under heavy rains in Georgia, Felix became ill and was hospitalized in a military hospital in Chattanooga, Tennessee. He returned to duty until General Robert E. Lee's surrender in 1865.

Sadao Munemori

Born in Glendale, California, Japanese American Sadao Munemori (1922–1945) enlisted in the US Army in February 1942 because he could not find employment as an auto mechanic due to racial discrimination. The military authorities weren't sure what to do with a Japanese American soldier on the mainland during the early months of World War II. By June 1942, the government formed the 100th Infantry Battalion from Nisei servicemen from Hawai'i. In 1943, the 100th became part of the newly formed all-Nisei 442nd Regimental Combat Team, and Sadao was sent to combat in Europe to replace fallen soldiers in the 100th Battalion. He participated in the rescue of the Lost Battalion, who were soldiers predominately from Texas, in France in 1944. In 1945, while in Italy, he was killed in action by jumping on a grenade to protect his squad. In spite of being a war hero, his family members were informed of his death while they were held in the Manzanar concentration camp in California. In 1946, immediately after World War II, Sadao became the only Nisei to be awarded the Congressional Medal of Honor, the nation's highest military award.

Sadao Munemori serving in WWII

Susan Ahn Cuddy

The first female Asian American naval officer and first female naval gunnery officer was Susan Ahn Cuddy (1915–2015). Born in Los Angeles, she grew up in a large household committed to helping Korean immigrants. Her parents, Dosan Ahn

52

Tammy Duckworth

Chang-Ho and Helen Ahn, were the first married Korean couple to immigrate to the United States in 1902. Her father, Dosan, was a leader in the movement for Korea to gain independence from Japan. He traveled to Asia for his activism work and died in prison in Korea in 1938. After America's entry into World War II, Susan signed up to join the navy in 1942 but was initially rejected because of her race. She persevered and was finally accepted into the first group of Women Accepted for Volunteer Emergency Service (WAVES). After intense training stateside, Susan worked as both a naval gunnery instructor and code breaker.

Tammy Duckworth

Tammy Duckworth (1968–) became the first US senator who was born in Thailand when she was elected by a wide margin to represent Illinois in 2016. The daughter of an American man who was an aid worker and a Thai woman of Chinese descent, Tammy joined the Army Reserve Officers' Training Corps (ROTC) while earning her master's degree in international affairs at George Washington University. While working on a doctorate at Northern Illinois University, she was called to active duty and lost both her legs in Iraq when her helicopter was shot down by a grenade. She was awarded a Purple Heart in 2004 while undergoing rehabilitation from her military injuries.

FILIPINO SOLDIERS IN WORLD WAR II

A day after the bombing of Pearl Harbor, Japanese military forces attacked the Philippines, an American commonwealth. Filipino soldiers, who were legally American nationals, were promised US citizenship and veterans benefits if they engaged in battle against the Japanese. Approximately 150,000 Filipinos were already living in Hawai'i and the US mainland during World War II. More than ten thousand of them fought in segregated units in the US Army.

The US government, however, broke their promises to the Filipino soldiers. Most of the 200,000 soldiers in the Philippines who fought for America did not receive their full GI Bill benefits and could not automatically become US citizens. A 1990 immigration reform bill finally awarded citizenship to World War II veterans, which at the time numbered 100,000. A program to facilitate the travel of family members from the Philippines to provide care for aging veterans in America is currently in place but has been in danger of being canceled.

IN THE SHADOW OF WAR

War in Asia often increased immigration of Asians to the United States. Some Japanese men decided to come to the United States to avoid fighting in the Russo-Japanese War (1904–1905). Forty-five thousand Japanese women who married American GIs during the occupation of Japan after World War II were given special permission to move to the United States with their husbands. The Korean War resulted in the emigration of fifteen thousand Koreans—specifically war brides, war orphans, academics, and businessmen. Under the leadership of President Gerald R. Ford, more than 120,000 refugees from Vietnam were allowed into the United States in the 1970s. Another 100,000 came from Cambodia and another 100,000 from Laos from 1979 to 1981.

The following Asian American writers, all born overseas, have told stories related to Asian immigrants dealing with the trauma of war while living in the US.

Velina Hasu Houston (1957–) was born in Tokyo and at age two was taken by her parents to live in Fort Riley, Kansas. Her Alabama-born Black father, who was also of the Blackfoot Pikuni tribe, met her Japanese mother while he was stationed in Japan after World War II. A holder of advanced degrees in

A scene from Velina Hasu Houston's play *Tea*

Viet Thanh Nguyen

writing and English, Velina is an award-winning playwright who has been inspired by her multicultural identity and Japanese heritage. *Tea*, the third play in a trilogy based on her family and her most well-known, debuted off Broadway at the Manhattan Theatre Club in 1987. It revolves around Japanese women like her mother who were "war brides," married to American soldiers of various races and ethnicities and residing in Kansas in the 1950s. In the play, four Japanese women gather to clean the home of a mutual friend who had died by suicide. Over tea, they share stories about the difficult and somewhat painful adjustment to a strange land and international marriage.

Chang-Rae Lee (1965–) has explored the Asian American immigrant experience through very different types of novels. Born in Seoul, he and his family immigrated to the United States from Korea when he was three years old. His 1995 debut novel was *Native Speaker*, an identity novel examining issues of language through a spy story. The protagonist is a second-generation Korean American named Henry Park, who is a company spy wrestling with his own feelings of cultural isolation when he investigates a Korean American city councilman in New York City. His second novel, *A Gesture Life*, follows the life of Franklin Sata, an immigrant physician who is haunted by his experiences as a medic for Korean women who were trafficked in Japan during World War II. And last of all, *The Surrendered* is a five-hundred-page book from the points of view of a Korean War refugee, an American GI, and an orphanage missionary.

In 2015, forty years after the end of the Vietnam War, Vietnamese American writer **Viet Thanh Nguyen** (1971–) released his debut novel, *The Sympathizer*, which won the Pulitzer Prize for Fiction and numerous other awards. Viet came to the United States as a refugee with his family in 1975 and, after spending time in a refugee camp in Fort Indiantown Gap, Pennsylvania, his family eventually moved to San Jose, where they opened a Vietnamese grocery store. Viet writes about the refugee experience in novels, short stories, and nonfiction. In *The Sympathizer*, a nameless Eurasian spy who has infiltrated the South Vietnamese Army arrives in Southern California to continue his work as a double agent within the refugee population. Viet is the first Asian American and Vietnamese American to serve on the Pulitzer Prize Board.

AAPI HEROES IN SCIENCE AND MEDICINE

Chien-Shiung Wu

Have you ever felt overlooked because of your gender? Chien-Shiung Wu (1912–1997), who is known as the "First Lady of Physics," felt that way when she worked in scientific research. Born in China, Chien-Shiung was encouraged by her father, an engineer and educator, and her teachers to research the power of radioactive isotopes. While the field was pioneered by another woman, Marie Curie, it was still a male-dominated community. Even though Chien-Shiung received her doctorate in physics in the United States, she discovered that many jobs were often closed to women. In 1944, she joined the government's Manhattan Project, which was created for the development of nuclear weapons during World War II. She played an important role in a theory involving beta decay, which happens when the nucleus of one element changes into another element. Two male physicists went on to win the Nobel Prize for this research in 1957, but Chien-Shiung was not included. She continued to work hard in her field, becoming the first woman to hold a tenured faculty position in Columbia University's physics department.

David Ho

Taiwan-born Dr. David Ho (1952–) has spent his career as a doctor helping patients who are sick with HIV and working to find a vaccine to cure the disease known as AIDS. He immigrated with his family to Los Angeles when he was in elementary

Chien-Shiung Wu working as a physicist

school. David went to public schools before attending Caltech and Harvard Medical School. While he was a young doctor at Cedars-Sinai Medical Center in Los Angeles, he treated patients, mostly young gay men, who were dying from HIV and AIDS. Soon, David and other medical professionals all over the world were working to figure out how they could help these patients. As the head of an AIDS research center in New York City, David and other researchers found an important

HIV treatment. They created a cocktail, or combination of drugs, that stopped HIV from growing. This helped keep patients healthy and prevented them from developing full-blown AIDS.

The Togasaki Sisters

The Togasaki sisters—six Nisei sisters from the same family, born in San Francisco from 1897 to 1908—were medical pioneers. They were inspired by their immigrant mother, who helped open a hospital for victims of the devastating San Francisco earthquake of 1906. The sisters each pursued a career in physically caring for others when Issei and Nisei people were often discriminated against. The oldest sister, Kazue Togasaki (1897–1992), and another Nisei, Megumi Shinoda, became the first women of Japanese ancestry to receive medical degrees in the United States in 1933. The second sister, Mitsuye Togasaki (1902–1973), was a public health nurse in Honolulu. Yoshiye Togasaki (1904–1999), the third sister, was the second Nisei accepted as an intern at the world-famous Los Angeles County General Hospital. Chiye Togasaki (1905–1990), the fourth sister, was a nurse and also served with her husband, Tamezo, at the Atomic Energy Commission in Hiroshima, Japan, after World War II. The fifth sister, Teru Togasaki (1907–1990), had a medical practice in Sacramento when Executive Order 9066 forced her into a concentration camp in Poston, Arizona. The sixth and youngest sister, Yaye Togasaki (1908–2005), became a psychiatric nurse with the Veterans Administration.

Patrick Soon-Shiong

Dr. Patrick Soon-Shiong (1952–) was a surgeon at UCLA where he treated pancreatic cancer patients. Unfortunately, the transplant surgeries were not working. He decided to research a new treatment that would only replace the bad cancer cells in the pancreas. He eventually created a new drug to treat pancreatic cancer and other types of cancer. He sold his companies for a lot of money and is now one of the richest doctors in the world. He also owns part of the Los Angeles Lakers professional basketball team and has bought two newspapers.

Patrick Soon-Shiong

ELECTORAL POWER

As the size of the Asian American population has dramatically changed since the 1960s, so too has its impact on elections. More than 13.3 million Asian Americans were eligible to vote in November 2022. A majority of them (57 percent) are naturalized citizens, meaning they were not born in the United States.

Both political parties have recognized the power of this fastest-growing group of eligible voters. The majority of eligible Asian American voters live in only five states—California, New York, Texas, Hawai'i, and New Jersey—but they can still be a deciding factor in close elections in other states.

Kamala Harris and her mother

Hiram L. Fong

THE FIRST ASIAN AMERICAN PRESIDENTIAL CANDIDATE

Hiram L. Fong (1906–2004) was born Yau Leong Fong to Cantonese-speaking immigrants in Honolulu, Hawai'i. As a speaker of the Hawai'i Territorial House of Representatives from 1948 to 1954, Hiram fought for Hawai'i to become a US state. A lawyer and businessman, he retired from politics for a short time before running for office after President Eisenhower signed a proclamation admitting Hawai'i as the fiftieth state. That year, in 1959, he became one of the two senators to represent the state. He was the first Asian American to serve in the US Senate. He remains the only Republican senator ever elected from Hawai'i. For eighteen years, Hiram advocated for civil rights and immigration reform that would benefit Asians. In 1964, he ran for the Republican Party's presidential nomination, making him the first Asian American presidential candidate.

BECOMING VICE PRESIDENT

Kamala Devi Harris (1964–) is also a political figure who represents many firsts. In 2021, she became the first woman and also first Black and South Asian person to be inaugurated as US vice president of the United States. She was born to two immigrant scholars: her late mother, Shyamala Gopalan, from Madras (now Chennai), India, and her Black father, Donald J. Harris, born in Jamaica. The couple met at a political protest while students at UC Berkeley. After their parents' divorce in the 1970s, Kamala and her sister, Maya, lived with their mother, whose breast cancer research took them to Canada. A lawyer, Kamala was elected district attorney of San Francisco in 2003, and seven years later, she was elected California's attorney general and oversaw the largest state justice

Fue Lee serving in the Minnesota House of Representatives

ranging in age from their twenties to forties, joined another Hmong American, **Fue Lee** (1991–), who had been in office since 2016, in the Minnesota House of Representatives. All are either refugees or children of refugees, concerned about the challenges people with similar backgrounds face in their everyday lives.

ASIAN AMERICAN VOTERS

A district in Southern California, the Forty-Fifth congressional district, has one of the largest Asian American electorates in the nation. It is near Los Angeles and its center is Little Saigon, in the historic center of the Vietnamese American community.

The 2022 election was between two Asian American candidates—Republican **Michelle Steel** and Democrat **Jay Chen**—showed that specific ethnicity of the candidates and voters can affect an election. Michelle, an experienced politician, is a Korean immigrant whose parents fled North Korea, while Jay is a Taiwanese American real estate investor and intelligence officer in the Naval Reserve. The election was close and, in the end, Michelle won with 52 percent of the vote.

department in the United States. She became a senator representing California in 2017 and served on the powerful Select Committee on Intelligence and the Judiciary Committee.

STATE REPRESENTATION

The political landscape of some areas in the United States has changed with both the increase of Asian Americans and their claim for self-determination.

This change began with Hawai'i when it was still a territory. Referred to as the Revolution of 1954, it was a huge transition that took place in the Territorial Legislature, which up until that time was ruled by white Republicans. Nisei soldiers who had served

in World War II returned to the islands, prepared to take a larger role in deciding their community's political future. Three decorated veterans—**Daniel Inouye**, **Spark Matsunaga**, and **George Ariyoshi**—all won seats in the territorial government and helped flip the legislature to Democrats. Daniel and Spark both went on to represent the state of Hawai'i in the US Senate while George became Hawai'i's first Japanese American governor and America's first governor of Asian ancestry.

More than seventy years later, another Asian American ethnic group rose to power—this time not on the warm islands in the Pacific, but in Minnesota with its freezing winter temperatures. In 2019, four Hmong Americans,

VOTING IN US TERRITORIES

Laws around voting in US territories can be confusing:

- American Samoans are considered US nationals but not US citizens.

- Guam elects one non-voting delegate to the House of Representatives. People born in Guam are considered US citizens but cannot vote in federal elections unless they move to one of the fifty states or the District of Columbia.

- Northern Marianas Islands are a commonwealth. Individuals born in the commonwealth are US citizens but cannot vote in presidential elections.

AAPI HEROES IN TELEVISION AND FILM

Sessue Hayakawa

Sessue Hayakawa (1886–1973) was a silent film star in the 1910s and 1920s. He had fans all around the world, including white Americans, despite his Japanese immigrant status. Sessue was able to come to the United States in 1907 with the help of his brother and other people from his village, who were fishermen in California. Sessue went to study at the University of Chicago but left to work at odd jobs and finally act in plays in Los Angeles's Little Tokyo, where he was discovered by Hollywood producers. His 1915 breakout role in *The Cheat* made him famous and he earned $2 million a year (the present-day equivalent of $28 million). He even created his own movie studio, Haworth Pictures. He often would star opposite white actresses, playing a forbidden lover or villain who rarely got the girl unless she was Japanese. When anti-Japanese sentiments grew after World War I, Sessue left Hollywood and toured Europe. He returned to the American screen after World War II and became the first Asian actor to be nominated for an Academy Award for his performance in *The Bridge on the River Kwai* in 1957.

Anna May Wong

When Los Angeles–born Chinese American Anna May Wong (1905–1961) was nine, she decided that she wanted to be a Hollywood movie star after watching silent films that were shooting around her family's laundry in Los Angeles's Chinatown.

Anna May Wong

She got her first break in the 1919 movie *The Red Lantern*, in which she was an extra and carried a lantern in one of the scenes. Her first leading role came when she was seventeen in *The Toll of the Sea* (1922), the first generally released film in color. Despite being in demand, Anna was frustrated that she was more often than not cast in either a supporting role or a stereotypical one. Because of anti-miscegenation laws, Anna could not play a romantic interest opposite a white leading man. Most insulting was when a big studio decided to cast white actors to play Chinese characters in the film adaptation of *The Good Earth*, Nobel Prize winner Pearl Buck's historical novel set in rural China. Anna created her own short-lived production company to more freely produce authentic projects that reflected her heritage. In her first and only trip to China in 1936, she directed and produced the documentary-like *My China Film*. She eventually went to Europe for better film roles. In 2023, Anna May Wong was on the face of the US quarter as part of the American Women Quarters Program.

Dwayne Johnson

Born in Hawai'i, Dwayne Johnson (1972–) followed in the footsteps of both his Samoan maternal grandfather and Black-Canadian father and pursued a successful career as "The Rock" in professional wrestling. He then moved into acting, becoming a movie star. He even created his own production company, Seven Bucks Productions. Dwayne was able to pay homage to his Samoan heritage when his character in *The Fast and the Furious* movie franchise returns to Sāmoa in the final scene.

Dwayne Johnson

Sandra Oh

When Sandra Oh (1971–), then a student at the National Theatre School of Canada, was cast as the lead in *The Diary of Evelyn Lau*, a Canadian television movie about a runaway, she knew that her life would change. On set, she got to know the actress Mina Shum, better known as a filmmaker, which led to another Canadian movie, *Double Happiness*, and other creative collaborations. Hollywood was less welcoming to this Korean Canadian actress at first, but she kept trying. She eventually landed a role on the TV show *Grey's Anatomy* as Dr. Cristina Yang. She won many awards for the role, including a Golden Globe. In 2018, Sandra became the first actress of Asian descent to be nominated for the Emmy Award for lead actress in a drama series for her role in the show *Killing Eve*. The same year, she became a naturalized US citizen and later described herself as an Asian Canadian American.

Ismail Merchant

Born Ismail Noormohamed Abdul Rehman in Bombay, India, Ismail Merchant (1936–2005) began his film career producing a short film, *The Creation of Woman*, which earned him an Oscar nomination. On his way to Europe for the Cannes Film Festival, he stopped in New York City and met a young director, James Ivory. The two of them fell in love and worked together on many movies, including the Oscar–nominated *Howards End*, *A Room with a View*, and *The Remains of the Day*. A devout Muslim, Ismail divided his time among Bombay, London, and two homes in New York.

Sandra Oh

BRUCE LEE AND THE LEGACY OF MARTIAL ARTS MOVIES

San Francisco–born Bruce Lee (1940–1973) was an international martial arts master. He broke the rules and pushed the limits of both kung fu and Hollywood, which helped to create more opportunities for people of Asian descent. Through his father, a Cantonese opera actor, he was in more than twenty Hong Kong movies by the time he was eighteen. When his parents sent him back to the United States, Bruce created his own kind of kung fu, Jeet Kune Do, which included techniques of other martial arts that he studied. He tried to make it big in American television and movies but was unable to because of anti-Asian discrimination. Bruce then returned to Hong Kong and created and starred in blockbuster martial arts movies, including *Enter the Dragon*. He was on his way to finally achieving his dreams in Hollywood when he unexpectedly died in Hong Kong at the age of thirty-two. He built a foundation for the success of future actors, including Jackie Chan and even Malaysia-born superstar Michelle Yeoh, whose film career began in Hong Kong martial arts movies.

Bruce Lee

Mindy Kaling

Mindy Kaling (1979–) was born in Cambridge, Massachusetts, and went to college at Dartmouth University. She majored in playwriting, did improv, and worked for the university's humor magazine. After graduating in 2001, she moved to New York City and worked as a production assistant for a TV show and did stand-up comedy gigs. Then she and her Dartmouth friend Brenda Withers produced an original two-woman play, *Matt & Ben*, in which Brenda played actor Matt Damon and Mindy played actor Ben Affleck. The play won multiple awards, and Mindy, an Indian American woman, found her way to Hollywood. She became the first woman of color to write and be on the hit TV series *The Office* and wrote more episodes than anyone else in the show's history. Next would be *The Mindy Project*, in which she starred as an obstetrician/gynecologist, like her late Mumbai-born mother, and executive produced for six seasons. She formed her own production company, Kaling International, and created more television shows with Asian American female characters.

Taika Waititi

MORE TV AND FILM HEROES

TYRUS WONG (1910–2016)
One of the most influential and celebrated Chinese American artists of the 20th century and the lead animator on the Disney movie *Bambi*

JAMES WONG HOWE (1899–1976)
A China-born American cinematographer who worked on over a hundred films and won two Academy Awards

DOMEE SHI (1989–)
China-born Canadian animator, director, and screenwriter is the first woman to solely direct a Pixar film (*Turning Red*)

KUMAIL NANJIANI (1978–)
Pakistani American actor, stand-up comedian, and screenwriter best known for the movie *The Big Sick* and his role as Kingo in the Marvel movie *Eternals*

Taika Waititi

The son of a Jewish educator and a Māori farmer and artist, Taika Waititi was born in New Zealand in 1975. The Māori people are Polynesians indigenous to New Zealand, meaning they were the first people to ever live there. They call New Zealand "Aotearoa."

After graduating from college in New Zealand, where he majored in theater, Taika was part of an award-winning comedy duo, the Humorbeasts. He then began to produce films primarily set in New Zealand and was able to make a breakthrough with his fourth independent film, *Hunt for the Wilderpeople*, which he filmed in his old school and grandmother's house. His creative playfulness led to a major project: He was selected to direct a Marvel blockbuster, *Thor: Ragnarok*, which premiered in 2017. Two years later, he won an Academy Award for adapting the book *Jojo Rabbit* into a movie.

ASIAN AND PACIFIC ISLANDER WORDS IN AMERICAN ENGLISH

The languages of Asia are very diverse. It's estimated that there are 2,300 languages spoken in Asia. The most popular Asian languages spoken at home in the United States today are Chinese (Mandarin and Cantonese), Tagalog (one of the Philippine languages), Vietnamese, Korean, and Hindi. Those are followed by Urdu and Gujarati (both languages spoken in India); Japanese; Telugu, Bengali, Punjabi, Tamil (these four are languages spoken in India); Hmong; and Khmer (the language of Cambodia).

Friends having fun while singing karaoke

DID YOU KNOW THAT THESE WORDS HAVE ASIAN AND PACIFIC ISLANDER ORIGINS?

Wikipedia—Hawaiian language: *wiki-wiki* for "fast"

Ketchup/catsup—Chinese: *kê-tsiap* for a type of Vietnamese sauce adopted by the Chinese

Boondocks—Tagalog: *bundók* for "mountain"

Karaoke—Japanese: *kara* for "empty" and *oke* for "orchestra." (Note: *Karate* in Japanese means "empty hand.")

Yo-yo—Tagalog for "come come" or "return"

THE YO-YO

Do you know that the name for the yo-yo has a connection to the Philippines through its creator, **Pedro Flores** (1896–1963)? Pedro grew up in the Philippines at a time when his birth country was experiencing great turmoil with the United States, which controlled the islands after signing a treaty with Spain. Pedro came to California in 1915 and, after dropping out of law school, began working as a bellhop in a hotel in Santa Barbara. During his lunch break, he carved a toy popular in the Philippines called a yo-yo or "come come" in Tagalog. He suspected that the yo-yo might catch on in America and at the age of twenty-nine, formed an official company that made thousands of yo-yos. During the depths of the Depression, he sold his company to businessman Donald E. Duncan. Today, the yo-yo is a general term with a very specific origin story.

Playing with yo-yos

PRONOUNCING COMMON ASIAN NAMES

With the vast variety of languages and regional distinctions, it is difficult to know how to pronounce certain Asian names. Also, ancestors who came early to America may have gone through the Angel Island immigration center in San Francisco and been given names by authorities in documents that did not correctly represent how they would like their names to be pronounced or spelled in English. When you are in doubt, just ask a person with an Asian name how they would like it to be pronounced.

Here are a few popular Asian first and last names and their common pronunciations:

Ng (Chinese)—ing

Nguyen (Vietnamese)—win

Watanabe (Japanese)—wata NAH-bae

Sok (Khmer)—sock

Bich (Vietnamese)—biet or bic

Phuc (Vietnamese)—fook

In some Asian countries, surnames, or last names, are more of a recent phenomenon. In Japan, commoners did not have last names until the Meiji Restoration, a political revolution that occurred in 1868. Names often refer to where ancestors lived or the type of work they did. Thai names can easily be changed to be unique from all non-relatives, thus resulting in very long last names. In contrast, over half of the population in South Korea are named either Kim, Park, or Lee.

AAPI HEROES IN MUSIC

Yo-Yo Ma playing the cello

Yo-Yo Ma

Cellist Yo-Yo Ma (1955–) is a musical legend who connects people with each other and the earth. Born to Chinese parents in Paris, at age seven, he performed a 150-year-old French composition in a cello-piano duet with his older sister, Yeou-Cheng, for President John F. Kennedy at the Kennedy Center in New York City. From that performance in 1962 to more than six decades following, Yo-Yo has gone on to record more than a hundred albums, including nineteen Grammy Award winners. In 1998, he created Silkroad, a group of international artists who combine their traditional instruments to make unique music. As a United Nations Messenger of Peace, he set out to perform Bach's six suites for solo cello in one sitting in thirty-six important locations throughout the world. In December 2022, Yo-Yo Ma joined members of the Polynesian Voyaging Society on a traditional canoe that represents the Hawaiian belief that everyone on earth is on the same journey.

Bruno Mars

Music superstar Bruno Mars (1985–), whose mother is from the Philippines, was born Peter Gene Hernandez, but at a young age was given the nickname Bruno by his Puerto Rican Jewish father. Bruno was onstage at a young age, performing as a mini-Elvis as part of his family's variety show, *Magic of Polynesia*, at the Hilton Hotel

The Linda Lindas

in Honolulu. He and his older brother traveled to Los Angeles to pursue their music. Bruno wrote songs with friends for other performers. After six years, Bruno received a big break as a performer with his debut single, "Nothin' on You," which topped the charts. Since 2009, he has produced hit after hit. Bruno followed his debut with four other No. 1 hits, a record that hadn't been matched since Elvis Presley.

The Linda Lindas

An anti-Chinese insult by a classmate inspired the young punk band the Linda Lindas to create the song "Racist, Sexist Boy." It was recorded at the Los Angeles branch library without an audience because of COVID-19. The video of their performance went viral on YouTube and other social media platforms, leading to a deal with a punk label, Epitaph. The Chinese-Latinx American band, comprised of two sisters (Lucia and Mila de la Garza), a cousin (Eloise Wong), and close friend (Bela Salazar), had already performed at fundraisers for Castelar Elementary School in Los Angeles's Chinatown. They also served as the opening musical act for established punk bands like Bikini Kill. The band was even in the Amy Poehler film *Moxie*, for Netflix. Within a year of the viral video release, the Linda Lindas were performing throughout the United States, Europe, and even Japan.

MORE MUSIC HEROES

HIROSHIMA
Grammy Award–winning jazz band that featured Japanese instruments like the koto and taiko

MICHELLE ZAUNER (1989–)
Korea-born American musician and lead singer of alternative pop rock band Japanese Breakfast, whose book, *Crying in H Mart*, was a *New York Times* bestseller

STEVE AOKI (1977–)
Japanese American DJ, music producer, and owner of the independent record label and lifestyle brand Dim Mak, named in honor of martial artist Bruce Lee's "death touch"

Israel Kamakawiwoʻole

Israel Kamakawiwoʻole

Israel Kamakawiwoʻole's version of the Judy Garland classic "Over the Rainbow" is simple: just the Native Hawaiian's sweet, melodic voice over the strumming of his ukulele. His version of the song, which is a medley with "What a Wonderful World," is the most popular of any other existing recording of the song. Honolulu-born Israel (1959–1997), his brother, and three other local Hawaiians formed a band called Mākaha Sons of Niʻihau in the 1970s to create a more authentic sound of the islands. In 1993, he released his first solo album, *Facing Future*, which featured the "Over the Rainbow/What a Wonderful World" medley, eventually making it the best-selling Hawaiian album ever. When Israel died in 1997, his body lay in state at the Capitol Building in Honolulu, reflecting the great love and respect the Hawaiian people had for the musician.

BEFORE K-POP

K-pop is pop music from South Korea. It was made popular in the United States by a Korean singing group called BTS. This hasn't been the first time Asian musicians made it in America. In the 1960s, there were the Kim Sisters from South Korea. The Kim Sisters are a group of two biological sisters and one adopted sister. A hit singing group among American GIs during the Korean War, the Kim Sisters eventually came to the United States to perform shows in Las Vegas and, later, on the *Ed Sullivan Show*, where they appeared twenty-two times. In 1962, their cover of the song "Charlie Brown" made it to No. 7 on the Billboard singles chart.

The oldest of the Kim Sisters, Sue, married in the US and performed in Las Vegas. In 2014, she became the first person of Korean descent to be inducted into the Nevada Entertainment/Artist Hall of Fame.

The Kim Sisters

LOVE FOR ELDERS

Many East Asian cultures are centered around the ancient teachings of the Chinese philosopher **Confucius**, who promoted the merits of filial piety, or respect for elders. In households with large extended families, grandparents may be especially cared for and at the heart of family gatherings. The family tree is very important and some cultures even have different names for grandpa and grandma, depending on whether they are from the mother's or father's side. Asian Americans are more likely than any other group to live in multigenerational family households. Two-thirds of Asian Americans say parents should have a lot or some influence in choosing one's job and spouse.

RESPECT FOR ELDERS

Because of this filial piety, altars for ancestors are often displayed in homes and places of business like a restaurant. Asian Americans may also practice regular tomb sweeping in which a family will go to clean an elder's gravesite, sometimes even leaving behind decorations. Incense can be lit and gifts of a favorite food can be left on the family altar beside a loved one's framed photograph. This practice is called *ancestor veneration* or *respect for elders* and does not necessarily have to be part of a religious practice.

Respecting elders at the family altar

NAMES FOR GRANDPARENTS IN SELECT ASIAN AND HAWAIIAN LANGUAGES

Chinese (Cantonese): Po Po (maternal grandma) and Gung Gung (maternal grandpa) / Mah Mah (paternal grandma) and Yeh Yeh (paternal grandpa)

Chinese (Mandarin): Lao Lao (maternal grandma) and Lao Ye (maternal grandpa) / Nai Nai (paternal grandma) and Ye Ye (paternal grandpa)

Tagalog: Lola (grandma) and Lolo (grandpa)

Korean: Halmoni/Halmeoni (grandma) and Harabeoji/Halabeoji (grandpa)

Hindi: Nani (maternal grandma) and Nana (maternal grandpa) / Dadi (paternal grandma) and Dada (paternal grandpa)

Vietnamese: Bà (grandma) and Ông (grandpa)

Japanese: Baachan (grandma) and Jiichan (grandpa)

Hmong: Niam Tais (maternal grandma) and Yawm Txiv (maternal grandpa) / Yawg (paternal grandma) and Pog (paternal grandpa)

Khmer: Yeay (grandma) and Ta (grandpa)

Hawaiian: Tutu wahine (grandma) and Tutu kane (grandpa) (or just Tutu for both)

(Tip: Search online to hear the actual pronunciations!)

CULTURAL PRACTICES AND SUPERSTITIONS

BABY TURNS ONE

When babies in traditional Korean American households are a year old, a special ceremony is held. Items representing various jobs are placed in front of them. The objects can include a book (scholar); pencil (writer); money (business and wealth); stethoscope (medical career); gavel (judge); ball (athlete); and yarn (long life and health).

The guests watch with excitement to see which items the baby grabs first, which foretells something about the baby's future career.

CANDY FOR MOURNERS

Depending on the family's religious beliefs, ancestry, and number of generations in the United States, Chinese Americans may choose to integrate certain cultural practices into a funeral, especially for an elder. In some instances, small white envelopes are prepared and distributed to funeral-goers as they leave. Inside could be a piece of candy and a quarter. Attendees are expected to eat the candy to remove the bitterness of the day. The quarter should be spent that day to pass along good fortune to others. There are many versions of this practice, but it always is meant to unify mourners.

INTERNATIONAL ADOPTION FROM ASIA

More than 150,000 children were adopted from Asia to other parts of the world between 1971 and 2001. They included mixed-race babies, girls from China, and both girls and boys from Korea and Vietnam. Many of them grew up in non-Asian families and communities in the United States. Older Asian American adoptees have formed groups to help younger ones understand their cultural roots and who they are in the United States.

Celebrating baby's first birthday

Not all Asian Americans or Pacific Islanders follow these practices, but many do!

- Remove shoes at the door of a house.

- Value lucky numbers such as 8. Many immigrant businesses in Chinese American communities use the number 8 in the name of their company.

- Native Hawaiian hā (breath): A traditional greeting in Hawaiʻi in which two people touch foreheads and share a breath.

AAPI HEROES IN BUSINESS AND HIGH TECHNOLOGY

Roger H. Chen

Roger H. Chen (1952–) is an immigrant from Taiwan who created an Asian food grocery chain in America during the 1980s. While in Southern California, he saw how many small food markets carrying Asian products were popular. He decided to open a large supermarket that sold Asian products. The company was at first called Tawa Supermarket, then was changed to 99 Ranch Market. The number 99 is a lucky number in Taiwan. In Mandarin, the number is related to longevity and good fortune. There are now more than fifty 99 Ranch supermarkets throughout the United States, including in Texas, Massachusetts, and New York.

Jawed Karim and Steve Chen

On April 23, 2005, the first YouTube video was uploaded by Bangladeshi-German American Jawed Karim (1979–). He is one of the three founders of YouTube. The video was called "me at the zoo" and showed twenty-four-year-old Jawed in front of the elephant habitat at the San Diego Zoo for nineteen seconds. A month later, another cofounder of YouTube, Taiwan-born Steve Chen (1978–), posted a video of his cat, Pajamas, which is the first cat video on YouTube. Jawed Karim, Steve Chen, and Chad Harley, the third cofounder, had all become friends while working for a different company and later came out with the idea of YouTube. Less than two years after its 2005 launch, YouTube became one of the most-visited destinations on the internet. Jawed,

Jawed Karim, Steve Chen, and Chad Harley

who can speak both German and Bengali, got his master's degree in computer science from Stanford University while Steve and Chad continued to work at YouTube. When YouTube was sold in 2009 to Google for $1.65 billion, all three cofounders became multimillionaires. In 2019, Steve moved his family to his birthplace, Taiwan, and is involved in helping to make Taiwan "Asia's Silicon Valley." Jawed has his own company called YVentures that puts money into other companies like Airbnb, Reddit, and Postmates. Jawed's first elephant video is the only post on his YouTube account, @jawed, and has more than 300 million views.

Bobby Murphy

Robert "Bobby" Murphy (1988–) is cofounder of Snapchat. He was born in California and his mother is from the Philippines. The son of California state employees, Bobby is a billionaire who made his fortune with his Stanford University fraternity brother, Evan Spiegel. Bobby and Evan created what they think of as an instant messaging app for friends. Snapchat, unlike the original posts of Facebook, Instagram, or Twitter, only shares pictures, videos, and messages for a short time before disappearing. As chief technology officer (CTO), Bobby oversees engineering and product development of the company. He is considered one of the most innovative CTOs to watch. He helped create filters on Snapchat so that a person's face can be distorted with masks and stickers. He is now one of the richest people in the world. Bobby and his wife, Kelsey Bateman, have donated $5 million to aid low-income individuals in Los Angeles who were hit hard by the pandemic.

Deborah "Deb" Yee-Ky Liu

Deborah Yee-Ky Liu

Deborah Yee-Ky Liu (1977–) is the president of the largest genealogical services company in the world, Ancestry.com. The daughter of Chinese immigrants, Deb grew up in a town in South Carolina where only 1 percent of the population was Asian. As her parents spoke only Chinese and ate Chinese food in the home, she was constantly teased and bullied for being different. Deb was smart and determined. She worked hard to attend college on a scholarship. She got her bachelor's degree in civil and environmental engineering from Duke University and her MBA from Stanford University. She worked almost six years at PayPal and then eleven years at Facebook before being offered the top position at Ancestry, a company that celebrates people's ethnic roots. She also cofounded a charity called Women in Product, and Deb has written a book to help women leaders in the business world.

Sundar Pichai, CEO of Google

Sundar Pichai

When Sundar Pichai (1972–) was growing up in his native Madras (now Chennai), India, he witnessed firsthand the power of technology. In the 1970s, phones were not easy to get in India. Sundar's household had to wait five years to get a rotary phone. Once his family managed to get a phone, they were able to do things like easily call a hospital to see if their medicine was ready instead of going on a two-hour round trip to check on it. Sundar also saw how technology could create community, as neighbors came to the Sundar home to use the phone. These kinds of experiences made him want to increase technological access to all people. He studied at the Indian Institute of Technology and received his master's degree in engineering and materials science from Stanford University and an MBA from the Wharton School of the University of Pennsylvania in 2002. He then got a job at Google, working to create its internet browser, Chrome, even though some people in the company thought it couldn't be made. Chrome now is the most-used web browser in the world. Sundar was named CEO of Google in 2015 and then of Google's new holding company, Alphabet, in 2019.

MORE BUSINESS AND HIGH-TECHNOLOGY HEROES

VINITA GUPTA (1950–)
India-born American businesswoman who was the first South Asian woman to start a publicly traded company in Silicon Valley

HANS GUNAWAN (1978–)
Indonesian American vice president of finance of Roblox, the hugely popular online gaming platform

SHAHID KHAN (1950–)
Pakistan-born American engineer and businessman who owns the global auto parts supplier Flex-N-Gate and the NFL team Jacksonville Jaguars

Albert Cheng

Albert Cheng

Albert Cheng (1970–) grew up on the island of Oʻahu in Hawaiʻi and loved to learn about mainland American culture through watching television. Like many relatives on his father's side of the family, he decided to pursue a career in engineering. He earned his material sciences and engineering degree at MIT and even got a job at Boeing. He was able to do the work but panicked because he didn't enjoy what he was doing. He even thought about becoming a lawyer before starting an MBA program at Harvard. There, he had summer internships in entertainment and discovered that his true passion lay in his childhood love of television. He worked at Disney, ESPN Networks, and Fox Cable Networks. The Taiwanese American is now the vice president and chief operating officer of Amazon Studios, in charge of all global creative and business operations for the $8 billion film and TV production and distribution company.

LET'S EAT

HOMEGROWN AND FOR SALE IN THE ASIAN MARKET

Favorite Asian vegetables and fruits are sometimes grown at home and shared with family and friends. They include bitter melon, persimmon, mikan (Japanese tangerine), loquat (a small Chinese fruit), and pomelo (a large grapefruit found in Southeast Asia). In Hawai'i, mango and papaya are grown on trees. Some fruits and vegetables, such as the large Korean pear, and ube, the Filipino purple yam, are sold in Asian markets.

RICE AND NOODLES

At the center of Asian American foods are rice and noodles. Nine out of the ten countries that consume the most rice are in Asia. In order, they are China, India, Bangladesh, Indonesia, Vietnam, the Philippines, Thailand, Myanmar (also called Burma), and Japan. (The tenth country is Brazil, where many Asians live.)

There are two basic types of rice. *Indica* is a long-grain rice that is grown in tropical places in Southeast Asia and South Asia. Among the long-grain rices are the aromatic types like jasmine or basmati, harvested and eaten in places like Thailand, Vietnam, Cambodia, India, and Pakistan. These aromatic grains tend to be fluffier when cooked. The *japonica* type of rice is sticky and either short or medium grain and is eaten in Japan, Korea, and North China. Japonica is used in sushi.

California Rice Production

The Sacramento Valley in the state of California is a large and important producer of japonica short-grain rice. This region, the same place where Chinese miners came during the gold rush, has the three elements ideal for growing rice: cold water from the Sierra Nevada, sunlight, and moderate temperatures cooled by ocean air.

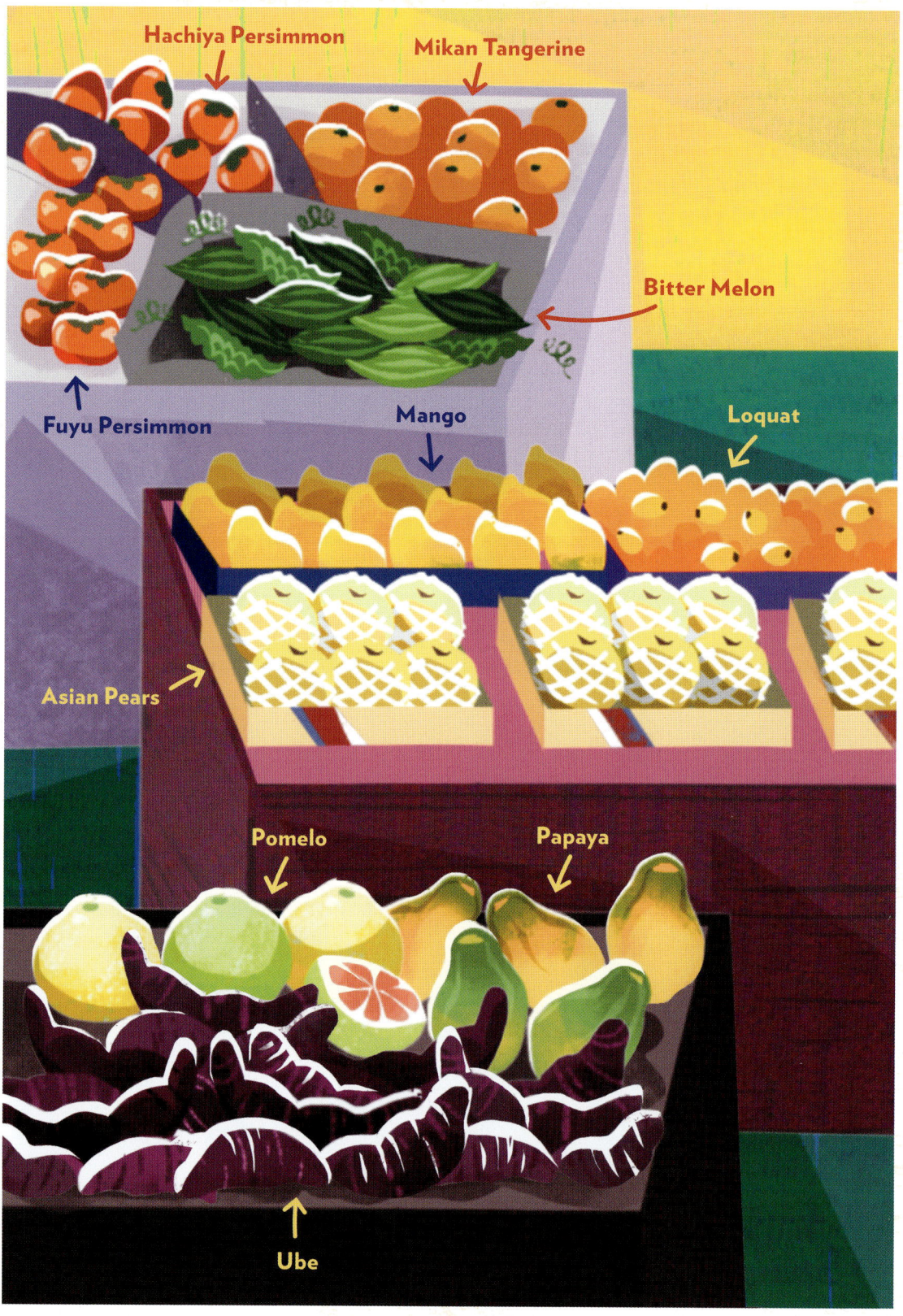

Hachiya Persimmon

Mikan Tangerine

Bitter Melon

Fuyu Persimmon

Mango

Loquat

Asian Pears

Pomelo

Papaya

Ube

Indica Rice

Japonica Rice

Chinese chopsticks

Vietnamese chopsticks

Korean chopsticks

Japanese chopsticks

Japonica was first grown in this area as a business in 1912. Later, a variety called Calrose was released and became the most popular rice among California farmers until the 1970s. A Japanese American family, the Kodas, operate the state's oldest family-owned and operated rice farm and mill.

Noodle Dishes

Noodles are also used in Asian cooking. Some are made from rice and others are produced from eggs. Popular Asian noodle dishes eaten in America include ramen, a Japanese soup with egg noodles that has roots in China and Korea; pho (pronounced "fuh"), a Vietnamese soup seasoned with fresh herbs in which usually rice noodles are used; pad thai, Thai rice noodles stir-fried with protein, peanuts, scrambled eggs, and peanuts; and chow mein, another stir-fry, but from Hong Kong and

mainland China, with egg noodles and various vegetables and meat, topped with a delicious gravy. Both the "men" in *ramen* and "mein" in *chow mein* are from the same Chinese root word, which means "noodle."

POI

Taro, also known as *kalo*, is a root vegetable that is sacred to Polynesian culture and a staple in its cuisine. Brown with bark-like texture on the outside, taro is shaped like a huge radish. Inside, its flesh is firm and cream colored. Many times, it can have purple flecks.

Taro is used in poi, a traditional starch in Native Hawaiian meals. It is steamed and then pounded and mashed into a thick, smooth liquid. Poi can be eaten by itself, sweetened, or seasoned with canned fish or other salty flavors.

NOT ONLY CHOPSTICKS

While East Asians such as the Chinese, Japanese, and Koreans may use chopsticks to eat, that is not the case for many other Asians. For instance, spoons and forks are the utensils of choice in Thailand, Cambodia, and Laos, whereas in South Asia and other Southeast Asian locations, hands are used. At one time, people in the Philippines also used their hands to eat, but after being colonized by Spain, they switched to the spoon and fork. Large spoons are preferred to scoop up soup and stews. In many Filipino households, giant wooden spoons and forks are placed on kitchen walls as decoration, representing the important role of eating together as a family and community.

POTLUCK

You've been invited to an Asian American potluck. What kinds of foods might you find there?

- Lumpia (Filipino egg rolls)

- Spam musubi (*musubi* means "roll" in Japanese. Here, slices of cooked Spam are used in place of fish or vegetables with sticky rice and nori, which is roasted seaweed. Spam became popular in Hawai'i and Korea because of US military bases.)

- Bao (Chinese steamed or baked buns filled with with meat or vegetables)

- Banh mi (Vietnamese sandwiches, dating back to the French colonization of Vietnam, that are made with baguettes)

- Chicken tikka (South Asian skewers flavored with masala spices)

- Kalbi (Korean short ribs)

Pad thai

Bao

Lumpia

Poi

Spam musubi

Ramen

Chicken tikka

Banh mi

Kalbi

AS AMERICAN AS . . .

There are popular foods and brands that Americans think came from Asia but actually were invented in the United States. In many cases, Asian Americans either invented the brand or made it popular in the United States.

GENERAL TSO'S CHICKEN

Similar to sweet and sour chicken but less sweet, comparable to Panda Express's orange chicken but hotter, General Tso's chicken is a dish more popular on the East Coast, particularly in New York City, where it was invented. Bits of chicken are fried in a batter and then covered in a sauce seasoned with ginger and chili peppers. People argue over what restaurant created it in the 1970s, as well as how the dish got its name. There was a real General Tso in Chinese history, but relatives in his hometown do not claim this American food invention.

CALIFORNIA ROLL

The origin of the California roll, a sushi roll that is usually wrapped around avocado and imitation crab, is also up for debate. There's no doubt that it was first created on the West Coast. Claims have been made that the California roll came from either Vancouver or Los Angeles. Most food historians believe it was invented by a Japanese immigrant sushi chef at a restaurant in Little Tokyo in the 1960s. The California roll is now popular all across the nation but still hasn't been fully accepted in Japan.

BUBBLE TEA

Bubble tea or boba is more than a drink; it's a culture of friendship that Asian Americans have even written songs about. In 2013, the Fung Brothers released the music video

From left, bubble tea, HI-CHEW, California roll, and General Tso's chicken

"Bobalife" on YouTube. It was filmed in the San Gabriel Valley, a section of Southern California known for its excellent variety of Asian restaurants, also called 626 after its telephone area code. Bubble tea was created in Taiwan in the late 1980s and originally consisted of tapioca balls (boba) in cold milk tea. It gained wide popularity among American high school and college students in the 2000s due to the influence of young Asian Americans in California. Today, bubble tea comes in multiple flavors and can be served with fruit.

HI-CHEW

HI-CHEW is a popular fruit-flavored candy, softer and chewier than Starburst, that was introduced from Japan to the United States in 2008. Now HI-CHEW can be seen in Major League Baseball dugouts and is endorsed by celebrities like Heidi Klum, John Mayer, and Ryan Gosling. Behind HI-CHEW is the pioneering Japanese candy company Morinaga. The founder, Taichiro Morinaga, moved to America at age twenty-three in 1888 and tasted Western candy for the first time. He returned to his home country and started selling his homemade candy from a pushcart. His product quickly took off, and his business grew into a huge candy-making empire. The Morinaga company invented an early version of the HI-CHEW in 1956. In 2015, the company opened a factory in North Carolina to make HI-CHEW.

AAPI HEROES IN FOOD

David Tran

Sriracha sauce and flavoring seem to be everywhere, but do you know that the brand in the clear rooster-logo plastic bottle with the green top was officially launched in Southern California in 1980? The founder of Huy Fong Foods, David Tran (1945–) was born in Vietnam in 1945 to an ethnic Chinese family. While in Vietnam, the family grew chili peppers. David began producing a red serrano hot sauce called *sriracha*, a traditional Southeast Asian seasoning named after a town in Thailand. During the Vietnam War, David and his family fled to the United States after a short time in Hong Kong. He named his company after the Taiwanese freighter that carried the Trans out of Vietnam. Even the rooster has a personal connection—David was born in the year of the rooster, according to the Chinese zodiac calendar. Huy Fong had humble beginnings in Los Angeles, but its sriracha quickly caught on, not from advertising but solely on the quality of the sauce.

Andrew Cherng and Peggy Cherng

How did orange chicken, a dish invented on American soil, become so popular? It goes back to a restaurant called Panda Express, which began serving Chinese food in Southern California in the 1980s under the leadership of Andrew Cherng (1947–) and Peggy Cherng (1947–). Andrew, the son of a Shanghai chef, was born in China, but also lived in Hong Kong, Taiwan, and Japan before immigrating to Kansas for college. Both he and Peggy, a Chinese native of Myanmar (also called Burma), earned advanced science degrees from the University of Missouri. The

David Tran, founder of Huy Fong Foods

Esther Choi

Cherngs leaned on the culinary know-how of Andrew's father and used the computer software and systems they learned in college to grow their business. Now Panda Express, the largest Asian restaurant chain based in the United States, is a multibillion-dollar family enterprise with restaurants around the world. The Cherngs are also active philanthropists, donating millions toward disaster relief, hospital care, and youth programs through the company's Panda Cares Foundation, as well as personally giving to nonprofits and institutions such as Caltech.

Esther Choi

In her early experiences in New Jersey, Esther Choi (1990–) cooked with her Korean grandmother, Jungok Yoo, and learned how to grow traditional ingredients and create base fermentation from scratch for kimchi and chili pastes. She later went to South Korea with her family for three years.

Upon returning to America, she began working part-time in restaurants starting at age fourteen. After receiving formal culinary training in New York City, she worked as a food buyer on multiple seasons of the TV show *Iron Chef*. At age twenty-eight, she opened her first restaurant, Mökbar, named after "mokbang," or the Korean television phenomenon of watching people eat. A finalist in the Netflix's *Iron Chef: Quest for an Iron Legend*, Esther has made appearances on

MORE FOOD HEROES

TED NGOY (1942–)
Cambodian American entrepreneur and former owner of a chain of doughnut shops in California

ROY CHOI (1970–)
A Korean American chef who ignited the street food culture with his Korean-Mexican taco business called Kogi

NIKI NAKAYAMA (1975–)
A Japanese American chef and the owner of Michelin-starred n/naka restaurant in Los Angeles that serves a traditional Japanese style of food called kaiseki, small dishes of perfectly calibrated flavors

David Chang

numerous cooking competitions, streaming shows, and YouTube programs. Zagat included Esther on their 30 Under 30 list and declared the gastropub named after her grandmother, Ms. Yoo, as one of New York City's hottest new restaurants. She also produces her own food products and hopes to release her own gochujang, Korea's trademark fermented red chili paste.

David Chang
Korean American David Chang (1977–) is sometimes known as a "bad boy" chef.

He is vocal about his mental health issues and drive for perfection in his *New York Times*–bestselling memoir, podcasts, and Netflix streaming series. His diverse background—he was born and raised in Arlington, Virginia; taught English in Japan; and attended culinary school in New York City—has informed his approach in pursuing unexpected deliciousness rather than hard-line authenticity. His love for ramen in Japan led him to open his restaurant, Momofuku Noodle Bar, in New York

City in 2004 with a $130,000 start-up investment from his father. Its success was followed by a significant expansion of his culinary empire, leading to David's multiple James Beard Awards and being named one of *Esquire*'s most influential people of the twenty-first century. He took a gamble on opening other restaurants and even a magazine, *Lucky Peach*, only to close some outlets and the magazine. These setbacks do not prevent him from continuing to take risks.

RELIGION AND RELIGIOUS PRACTICES

Asian Americans are not as religious as the general population. In one survey, only 39 percent say that religion is important to them, as compared with 58 percent of the American public. For example, about half of Chinese Americans are not connected with any religion.

Religious Asian Americans follow diverse faiths. Most Filipinos are Catholic, about half of Indian Americans are Hindu, most Koreans are Protestant, and most Americans of Vietnamese Cambodian, and Thai descent are Buddhist. Bangladeshis and Pakistanis tend to be Muslim. With Japanese Americans, 38 percent are Christian and 25 percent are Buddhist.

Temples in the United States can also be gathering places for festivals that are open to the public.

Catholic, Protestant, and Mormon missionaries were active in the Pacific Islands; and because of that, most Pacific Islanders follow one of those three faiths, or a mixture of those faiths with native spiritual practices.

A Buddhist temple celebration

CHINESE ZODIAC

Based on the year you were born, you are given a certain animal sign according to the Chinese zodiac system. Many other Asian cultures also follow the Chinese zodiac. There are a total of twelve animals that repeat every twelve years. When a person turns sixty, the Chinese believe that a cycle has been completed and life begins again.

What animal are you?

*Vietnamese zodiac has a water buffalo instead of an ox and a cat instead of a rabbit.

OX/WATER BUFFALO*
2033
2021
2009
1997
1985

RAT
2032
2020
2008
1996
1984

TIGER
2034
2022
2010
1998
1986

RABBIT/CAT*
2035
2023
2011
1999
1987

DRAGON
2036
2024
2012
2000
1988

SNAKE
2037
2025
2013
2001
1989

HORSE
2038
2026
2014
2002
1990

RAM
2039
2027
2015
2003
1991

MONKEY
2040
2028
2016
2004
1992

ROOSTER
2029
2017
2005
1993
1981

DOG
2030
2018
2006
1994
1982

PIG
2031
2019
2007
1995
1983

CELEBRATIONS AND FESTIVITIES

There are a number of Asian American and Pacific Islander festivals held in the United States. Some festivals are unique to America and have been around for more than one hundred years.

NEW YEAR

The new year is the most important holiday in many Asian cultures. Japan is one of the few Asian nations that mark the new year according to the Gregorian calendar, or January 1. Mochi, pounded rice balls, is traditionally served in Japanese households in a special soup called *ozoni*. Hmong New Year, on the other hand, is usually celebrated at the end of the year to mark the harvest season. Thai New Year, or Songkran, is celebrated in Los Angeles in August, but it is usually observed in April.

LUNAR NEW YEAR

Most other Asian ethnic groups observe the lunar calendar, based on the phases of the moon. Americans are probably most familiar with Lunar New Year festivals and parades in Chinese immigrant communities. Within families, elders usually give children money in red envelopes, sometimes referred to as *lucky money*. Among the cities hosting the largest Lunar New Year celebrations are San Francisco, New York City, Chicago, Houston, Boston, Spokane, and Los Angeles.

A Chinese Lunar New Year parade

LUNAR FESTIVALS

There have been a growing number of Vietnamese Tet (lunar) festivals as well. One of the largest festivals is held in Orange County by the Union of Vietnamese Student Associations of Southern California.

There is the Full Moon Festival or Mid-Autumn Festival, during which moon cakes, thick pastries with different fillings, are sold and eaten. Night markets, popular in Taiwan and Thailand, can now be found in the United States. The 626 Night Market was one of the first organized groups to hold events in

Southern California featuring various Asian foods served in individual booths. The number 626 refers to the telephone area code in the San Gabriel Valley, the center of the best Asian foods in the nation. The Queens Night Market in New York City was launched in 2015.

A Vietnamese Tet (lunar) festival

OTHER CELEBRATIONS

Besides new year festivals, the following are a sampling of other celebrations open to the American public:

East

KOREAN HARVEST AND FOLKLORE FESTIVAL
in Ridgefield Park, New Jersey

. . . .

Organized by the Korean Produce Association in early October

Midwest/South

APIDA ARTS FESTIVAL
in Chicago, Illinois

. . . .

Celebration of the creativity of Asian, Pacific Island, and Desi/South Asian Americans in Chicago in May. apidaarts.org

ASIAN FESTIVAL
in Columbus, Ohio

. . . .

A dragon boat race, Asian Games, and festival held in May to mark Asian Pacific American Heritage Month. asian-festival.org

DETROIT CHINA FESTIVAL
in Detroit, Michgan

. . . .

Largest Asian-themed event in Detroit in September featuring Chinese street food and music. detroitchinatownllc.com/event/

FESTIVAL OF LIGHTS
in San Antonio, Texas

. . . .

One of the largest celebrations of Diwali, India's Festival of Lights, in honor of San Antonio's sister city, Chennai, India. visitsanantonio.com/diwali-san-antonio

Diwali, India's Festival of Lights

COLORADO DRAGON BOAT FESTIVAL
in Denver, Colorado

. . . .

The largest dragon boat race in the United States. Includes food booths and an Asian marketplace. cdbf.org

NISEI WEEK JAPANESE FESTIVAL
in Los Angeles, California

. . . .

Established in 1934 and usually held in August, this is one of the longest-running ethnic festivals in the United States. niseiweek.org

OKINAWAN FESTIVAL
in Hawaiʻi

. . . .

Started in 1982 by the Hawaii United Okinawa Association, this festival celebrates all things Okinawan and brings together Okinawans and Okinawans at heart. okinawanfestival.com

PISTAHAN PARADE
in San Francisco, California

. . . .

The largest Filipino parade on the West Coast, produced by the Filipino American Arts Exposition (FAAE). pistahan.net

PRINCE KŪHIŌ HOʻOLAULEʻA AND PACIFIC ISLAND FESTIVAL
in Henderson, Nevada

. . . .

Held in partnership with the Las Vegas Hawaiian Civic Club at Water Street Plaza next to the Henderson city hall in September.

Nisei Week Japanese Festival

ALOHA FESTIVAL
in Waikīkī, Oʻahu, Hawaiʻi

· ·

This is the largest Hawaiian
cultural celebration in the United States.
alohafestivals.com

91

AAPI MUSEUMS AND PLACES OF INTEREST

East

Asia Society
725 Park Avenue
New York, NY 10021
asiasociety.org/new-york

Chinese American Museum
1218 16th Street Northwest
Washington, DC 20036
chineseamericanmuseum.org

Korean Cultural Center NY
460 Park Avenue, 6th Floor
New York, NY 10022
koreanculture.org

Museum of Chinese in America
215 Centre Street
New York, NY 10013
mocanyc.org

National Museum of Asian Art
1050 Independence Avenue SW
Washington, DC 20560
asia.si.edu

Smithsonian Asian Pacific American Center
600 Maryland Avenue Southwest
Washington, DC 20024
smithsonianapa.org

Midwest/South

Asia Society Texas
1370 Southmore Boulevard
Houston, TX 77004
asiasociety.org/texas

Chinese American Museum of Chicago
238 West 23rd Street
Chicago, IL 60616
ccamuseum.org

Japanese American Service Committee
4427 North Clark Street
Chicago, IL 60640
jasc-chicago.org

Korean Cultural Center of Chicago
9930 Capitol Drive
Wheeling, IL 60090
kccoc.org

Mississippi Delta Chinese Heritage Museum
Delta State University
1003 West Sunflower Road
Cleveland, MS 38732
chineseheritagemuseum.org

Morikami Museum and Gardens
4000 Morikami Park Road
Delray Beach, FL 33446
morikami.org/

Shraman South Asian Museum and Learning
    Center Foundation
2700 West Plano Parkway
Plano, TX 75075
shraman.org

West and Hawai'i

Bainbridge Island Japanese American
    Exclusion Memorial
4192 Eagle Harbor Drive Northeast
Bainbridge Island, WA 98110
bijac.org

Chinese American Museum
425 North Los Angeles Street
Los Angeles, CA 90012
camla.org

Chinese Historical Society of America
965 Clay Street
San Francisco, CA 94108
chsa.org

Filipino American National Historical Society
810 18th Avenue, Room 100
Seattle, WA 98122
fanhs-national.org

Filipino American National Historical Society
    Museum
337 East Weber Avenue
Stockton, CA 95202
fanhsmuseum.com

Golden Spike National Historic Park
6200 North 22300 West
Promontory, UT 84307
nps.gov/gosp

Japanese American National Museum
100 North Central Avenue
Los Angeles, CA 90012
janm.org

Ka'iwakīloumoku Hawaiian Cultural Center
Pacific Indigenous Institute
1887 Makuakāne Street
Honolulu, HI 96817
kaiwakiloumoku.ksbe.edu

Korean Cultural Center
5505 Wilshire Boulevard
Los Angeles, CA 90036
kccla.org

Manzanar National Historic Site
5001 Highway 395
Independence, CA 93526
nps.gov/manz/index.htm
Marshall Gold Discovery State Historic Park
Highway 49 between Placerville and Auburn
Coloma, CA 95613

Pacific Island Ethnic Art Museum
695 Alamitos Avenue
Long Beach, CA 90802
pieam.org

San Diego Chinese Historical Museum
404 Third Avenue
San Diego, CA 92101
sdchm.org

USC Pacific Asia Museum
46 North Los Robles Avenue
Pasadena, CA 91101
pacificasiamuseum.usc.edu

Wing Luke Museum of the Asian Pacific
American Experience
719 South King Street
Seattle, WA 98104
wingluke.org

FURTHER LEARNING

Books

Chang, Michael with Mike Yorkey. *Holding Serve: Persevering On and Off the Court.* Nashville: Thomas Nelson, 2002.

Hirahara, Naomi. *We Are Here: 30 Inspiring Asian Americans and Pacific Islanders Who Have Shaped the United States.* New York City: Running Press Kids, 2022.

Lee, Erika and Judy Yung. *Angel Island: Immigrant Gateway to America.* New York City: Oxford University Press, 2010.

Nguyen, Dat with Rusty Burson. *Dat: Tackling Life and the NFL.* College Station, Texas: Texas A&M University Press, 2005.

Shively, Carol A., ed. *Asians and Pacific Islanders and the Civil War,* Washington: National Park Service, 2015.

Uno, Roberta, ed. *Unbroken Thread: An Anthology of Plays by Asian American Women.* Amherst: University of Massachusetts Press, 1993.

Multimedia

Melissa Block and Elissa Nadworny, "The Legacy of the Mississippi Delta Chinese," March 18, 2017, in *Weekend Edition Saturday*, produced by Elissa Nadworny, audio, 5:25, https://www.npr.org/2017/03/18/519017287/the-legacy-of-the-mississippi-delta-chinese.

INDEX

ENJOY THE REST OF THE CHILD'S INTRODUCTION SERIES!

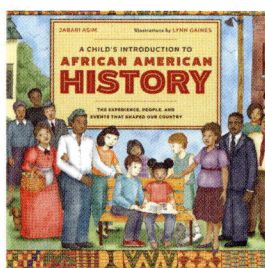

A Child's Introduction to African American History

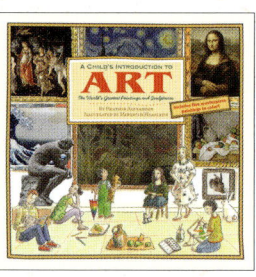

A Child's Introduction to Art

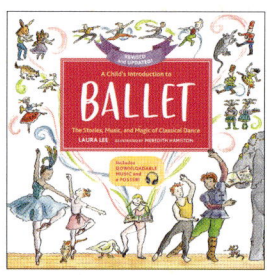

A Child's Introduction to Ballet

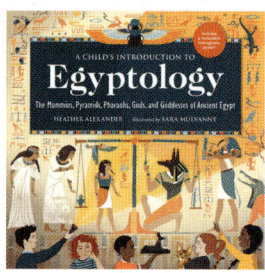

A Child's Introduction to Egyptology

A Child's Introduction to the Environment

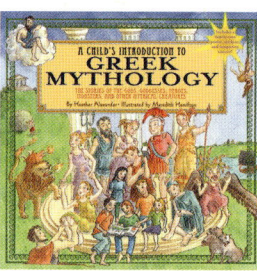

A Child's Introduction to Greek Mythology

A Child's Introduction to Hip-Hop

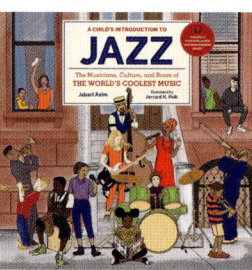

A Child's Introduction to Jazz

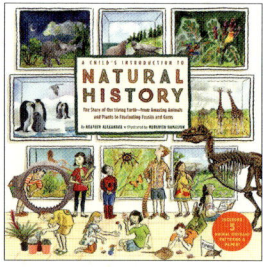

A Child's Introduction to Natural History

A Child's Introduction to the Night Sky

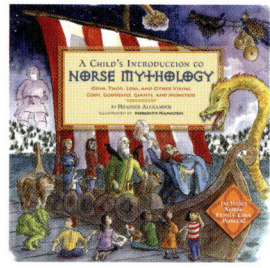

A Child's Introduction to Norse Mythology

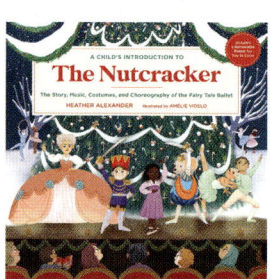

A Child's Introduction to *The Nutcracker*

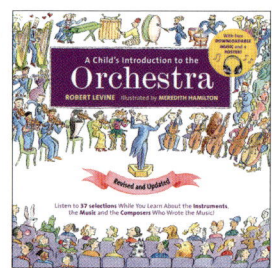

A Child's Introduction to the Orchestra

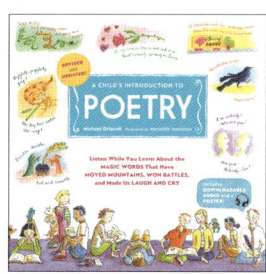

A Child's Introduction to Poetry

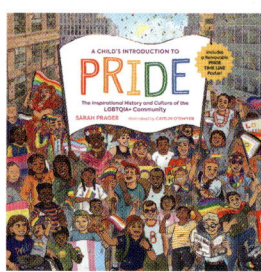

A Child's Introduction to Pride

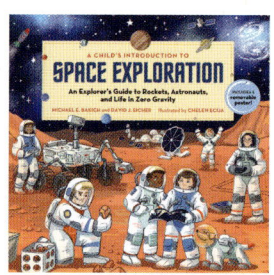

A Child's Introduction to Space Exploration

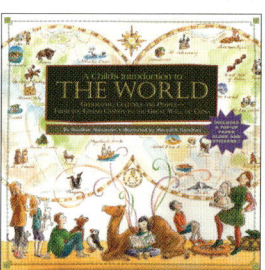

A Child's Introduction to the World